Praise for *Momentum for Life,*
Revised Edition

"Michael Slaughter is more than a church leader—he's a visionary whose writing is informed by extensive life experience and a deep sense of personal mission. In this revised edition of *Momentum for Life*, Michael makes his practices of self-leadership accessible to a younger and broader audience than ever before. My old rule still applies: read anything and everything written by Michael Slaughter!"

—**Jim Garlow**, Senior Pastor, Skyline Church, San Diego

"In sports, everyone understands the power of momentum! In life, the same force is at work. A great life doesn't just happen—but if you are serious about real life change, about having a deep relationship with God, about living with passion and purpose, about living a life that matters, then this book is for you. You will be challenged and revitalized to be at your best in all aspects of life—spiritually, physically, and relationally!"

—**Jimmy Page**, Fellowship of Christian Athletes, Executive Director for Health & Fitness Ministry

"If you feel stuck spiritually or physically and are wondering what God really has in mind for you, I encourage you to read this book. Warning: This is not a book of ways to get you off the hook but rather a deep discovery of yourself. If you are ready to finally move ahead and eager to experience the greatness God has in store for you, then pick up a copy today!"

—**Lorraine Bossé-Smith**, Author of *Leveraging Your Leadership Style, Finally Fit,* and *Fit Over 50*

"Everyone of us wants to make our life count and make a difference. . . . From his own personal experiences involving marriage, commitment to Christ, and his health, Slaughter outlines his personal journey in not just avoiding disaster but living life to the max."

—**John Ed Mathison**, Senior Pastor, Frazer Memorial United Methodist Church, Montgomery, Alabama

"Want to know the secrets to living a full, Christian life? Then devour this book."

—**Bill Easum**, Church Consultant and Author of

D1051201

Other Books by Michael Slaughter

Spiritual Entrepreneurs:
Six Principles for Risking Renewal
(Abingdon Press, 1995)

Out on the Edge:
A Wake-Up Call for Church Leaders
on the Edge of the Media Reformation
(Abingdon Press, 1998)

Real Followers:
Beyond Virtual Christianity
(Abingdon Press, 1999)

Money Matters:
Financial Freedom for All God's Children
(Abingdon Press, 2006)

Money Matters:
Financial Freedom for All God's Churches
(Abingdon Press, 2006)

UnLearning Church: New Edition
(Abingdon Press, 2008)

michael slaughter

momentum
for life
revised edition

Biblical Principles for Sustaining Physical Health, Personal Integrity, and Strategic Focus

Abingdon Press
Nashville

MOMENTUM FOR LIFE
BIBLICAL PRINCIPLES FOR SUSTAINING PHYSICAL HEALTH, PERSONAL INTEGRITY,
AND STRATEGIC FOCUS, REVISED EDITION

This book is printed on acid-free paper.

Library of Congress Cataloging-in-Publication Data

Slaughter, Michael.
   Momentum for life : biblical principles for sustaining physical health, personal integrity, and strategic focus / Michael Slaughter with Warren Bird and Kim Miller.—Rev. ed.
      p. cm.
   ISBN 978-0-687-65009-5 (binding: pbk., adhesive, perfect : alk. paper)
   1. Leadership—Religious aspects—Christianity. 2. Christian leadership. 3. Leadership. I. Bird, Warren. II. Miller, Kim, 1956– III. Title.

BV4597.53.L43S53 2008
253—dc22

2008002008

08 09 10 11 12 13 14 15 16 17—10 9 8 7 6 5 4 3 2 1
MANUFACTURED IN THE UNITED STATES OF AMERICA

To my nine young heroes—Thomas Beechem, Matt Cermak,

Jon Crawford, Kelsey Francis, Anna Mathias, Jason Meyer,

Erica Prigg, Jonathan Slaughter, and Ann Marie Wainscott—

who are running the race of faith

with the passion and endurance to win

contents

Acknowledgments ix

1. Momentum: Mass in Motion 1

2. **D**evotion to God 27

3. **R**eadiness for Lifelong Learning 47

4. **I**nvesting in Key Relationships 67

5. **V**isioning for the Future 85

6. **E**ating and Exercise for Life 107

7. Work Your Program: Thriving in Life, Influence, and Mission . . . 125

Appendix: Resources to Keep You Growing 131

Notes 133

acknowledgments

I am indebted to the great cloud of witnesses who have surrounded my life with models for living, many of whom are named in the pages of this book with specific examples of their impact. I especially want to thank my family: my wife, Carolyn, my daughter and son-in-law, Kristen and Brendan, and my son, Jonathan, who have embraced the disciplines of momentum for their lives as well. I give thanks for Pastor Wayne Cordeiro, New Hope Christian Fellowship O'ahu, who triggered the idea that led to Ginghamsburg's *Transformation Journal* mentioned throughout this book.

Kim Miller, creative director at Ginghamsburg, partners with me in worship design as well as book design and has tirelessly nurtured God's heartbeat for this work. She, along with the other members of Ginghamsburg's senior management team—Pastors Sue Nilson Kibbey and Mike Bowie, along with John Jung, Karen Smith, Nate Gibson, and Bruce Denlinger—support me in ways that enable me to put focus on what I do best at Ginghamsburg. Numerous support personnel also contributed to the creation of this book, including Todd Carter, Michael Pollard, Penny Powers, Brad Wise, Dwayne and Kay Ann Wilson, and the servants on Ginghamsburg's Internet team headed by Mark Stephenson.

Warren Bird, collaborative author and longtime friend, arranged my written outlines into flowing paragraphs, filled in missing pieces, and offered valuable content suggestions. Thanks also go to Rob Simbeck for his many hours updating the book for this revised edition.

The dedication page of this book credits a rising generation. Their momentum for life exceeds my own, and God will do far greater things through them as a result.

momentum:
mass in motion

MOMENTUM> *Mass in motion. Quantity of forward
motion. Impetus. For example: "A team that has
momentum is on the move and hard to stop."*

*I rejoiced with those who said to me, "Let us go to the house
of the LORD." (Ps. 122:1)*

For all its storied history, the World Series rarely captures my attention. Most years I've forgotten who has won by the time the next
spring training rolls around.

Don't get me wrong—I am a lifelong baseball enthusiast. All the boys
I knew growing up in Cincinnati in the 1950s and 1960s were baptized in
sauerkraut, German beer, and baseball. A trip with my dad to see young
Frank Robinson send one downtown in old Crosley Field was truly a tran-
scendental experience.

There is just one problem with the World Series—my hometown team
is usually not in it, so come October I turn my attention to more pressing
matters.

There was something different, though, about the series of 2004. The
Boston Red Sox had a history of coming up one short. They had not won
a series since 1918, after which they traded Babe Ruth to the New York
Yankees. Between 1918 and 2003 the Sox appeared in only four World
Series, losing each in game seven. Their almost-victory in 1986 was a clas-
sic study in futility. One out away from a long-awaited championship, they
and history watched as a ground ball rolled through first baseman Bill
Buckner's legs and into right field. Buckner hadn't gotten his glove low
enough, the ball rolled by, and the Mets scored the series-winning run.

The curse of the Bambino (as people called it) seemed to strike again
in 2004 as the Sox fell to the mighty Yankees in the first three games of
the American League play-offs. No team had ever come back after being

A team that has momentum is on the move and hard to stop.

down three games to none. Boston would need to win four games straight, the last two of them in Yankee Stadium.

The Red Sox won games four and five, and then I turned on my television. There was a growing confidence in the eyes of the players as they traveled to New York for the sixth game of the series. It appeared that momentum had begun to turn in their direction, and a team that has momentum is on the move and hard to stop.

Boston went on to accomplish what no other team in the history of baseball ever has. They won the championship series against the Yankees after being down three games to none, and then swept the St. Louis Cardinals in four straight games to win the World Series.

Momentum for Life

Every baseball team goes into the season with the goal of reaching the Series and winning the prize. Some teams break out early, only to fade in the heat of August. Others persist, however, paying the patient daily dues of disciplined practice on the fundamentals.

Likewise, you cannot get where you want to be in your faith, influence, relationships, vocation, or physical-emotional health if you are not moving forward. From priests to presidents the landscape is littered with the corpses of talented people who failed to maintain the positive momentum of character development.

All progress, all positive influence, begins with self-leadership.

Leaders and influential people have failed all around us, from the military command at Abu Ghraib prison to those behind the *USA Today* plagiarism scandal. From Bill Clinton's indiscretions to Martha Stewart's deceptions, from the executive failure at Enron to the high-tech meltdown

You cannot get to where you want to be in your faith, influence, relationships, vocation, or physical-emotional health if you are not moving forward.

—people of influence in government, business, and religion alike stumble into the oblivion of moral and ethical failure.

Many church problems trace back to such failures as well. They show up in the Catholic sex-abuse scandal and its widespread cover-up. They're evident when the president of a major Protestant denomination admits to an extramarital affair and is jailed for financial misdealing. And what is true for people in the news is true for all of us. Maintaining life-momentum is imperative if we are going to navigate our way faithfully through a world of clouded moral boundaries.

> **Maintaining life-momentum is imperative if we are going to navigate our way faithfully through a world of clouded moral boundaries.**

What's more, we are all people of influence. We are all real or potential leaders. Each of us has an effect on those in our circles of acquaintance, a bigger effect on our circles of friends and colleagues, and a still bigger one on our family members. Those of us who are parents are in a position of profound influence—even during those years when we're sure our children aren't listening! Influence is more often about our actions than our words, and it can be negative or positive. Kind words and angry words, conscientious work and slipshod work—each can cause ripples that extend much farther than we can see. That means the integrity we bring to each action is vital, for it sets in motion events we often don't foresee, no matter who we are.

You may recall the 2004 scandal in which an independent review revealed the false report given on the program *60 Minutes* concerning President George W. Bush's National Guard service. The failure to follow the disciplined procedures of faithful reporting resulted in the firing of three news executives and a producer. The incident no doubt also influenced the timing of Dan Rather's announcement that he would soon step down as anchor of the *CBS Evening News*. Not exactly the footnote that you want on your obituary after a long, illustrious career! These newsmen didn't seem to realize that all leadership begins with self-leadership.

> **All leadership begins with self-leadership.**

Settling for Lesser Dreams

We dream about the incredible opportunities that we have to influence the world for God's purpose. We know that through God's Spirit we can make lasting contributions that benefit the well-being of others. But *having a dream* and having the disciplined, lifelong dedication to *realize that dream* are two different things. It is easy to make a commitment, but keeping that commitment for life is another matter.

When I was in seminary, I hung out with five guys. We were drawn to one another because in our pre-Christian lives all of us had lived large and lived lost. Each of us had known some form of major failure, ranging from academic frustrations to chemical addictions. Each of us had experienced a new life "calling" and wanted passionately to be used by God in major ways. All of us were married and voicing our commitment to make our marriages last a lifetime.

Things haven't turned out the way we planned. Today only two of the five are still married to the same woman and both of us endured years of marital crisis, which we survived only by God's grace.

Most good things don't happen magically or suddenly. They are the result of a predetermined desire, an ongoing commitment to build momentum for life. Faith is not an instant realization of a desired future, for nothing worthwhile can be acquired at once.

> Now faith is being sure of what we hope for and certain of what we do not see. (Heb. 11:1)

Many young people start with dreams of walking closely with God and being used to make a difference on planet Earth. As I invest the second half of my life in training young leaders, however, I see bright, rising stars tempted to compromise their idealistic visions by age thirty. They begin to work for money instead of meaning. They settle for a job instead of a life calling. They focus their lives on personal achievement rather than on enduring contributions.

I see bright, rising stars tempted to compromise their idealistic visions by age thirty, working for money instead of meaning.

Young people are selling out and older people are cashing out.

God wants so much more. God wants to build lifelong momentum toward what we were created to become. The Apostle Paul compares the life of faith to running a race that requires the impetus of momentum.

> Do you not know that in a race all the runners run, but only one gets the prize? Run in such a way as to get the prize. Everyone who competes in the games goes into strict training. They do it to get a crown that will not last; but we do it to get a crown that will last forever. Therefore I do not run like someone running aimlessly; I do not fight like a boxer beating the air. No, I strike a blow to my body and make it my slave so that after I have preached to others, I myself will not be disqualified for the prize. (1 Cor. 9:24-27)

Instead of climbing to new heights, too many people plateau when they meet resistance. It doesn't have to be that way. God wants to win the battle for the soul of the world, and it begins for each of us with the management of the world inside. I've learned this the hard way through several conversionlike crises:

- My *marriage*. On June 1, 1992, my wife, Carolyn, and I made the disciplined commitment to start our marriage over. After almost twenty years together we were headed toward divorce. Instead, I had a conversion about investing in that key relationship.
- My *devotion*. On August 17, 1994, I traveled to Korea with a doctor of ministry class from a nearby seminary. As we learned firsthand about the amazing revival sweeping that country, I saw that the real power was in the Korean church's commitment to prayer. I made the disciplined commitment to begin every day with a time of devotional meditation and prayer.
- My *body*. On August 18, 2000, I was at a restaurant and started to feel sick. Seconds later I collapsed and was rushed to the hospital. In the days that followed, a cardiologist said I hadn't taken good care of my heart and body. My body fat content was in the 30s—a ridiculously high level—so in October 2000 I started working with a personal trainer. I was converted in the way I eat and exercise.

In the wake of these potentially catastrophic events and my accompanying mini-conversions, I had a breakthrough. I discovered a group of practices that helped me achieve a self-discipline I had not experienced before. These practices cover every key area of my life—spiritual, intellectual, interpersonal, physical, and missional—so that when I follow them faithfully I am a more complete human being. The opposite is also true—when I neglect any one of them, I begin to plateau and lose momentum. Worse, I begin to downsize God's dream.

These practices enable me to build momentum for life. They keep me on an upward climb. My belief that they can be useful to you is at the heart of this book. I am convinced that every follower of Christ needs to find self-management practices that create momentum for life. Mine are based on the acronym D-R-I-V-E. They are the elements that keep me moving with momentum toward God's promised future, and I believe they can be effective tools for you as well.

Devotion

D stands for devotion. This is the spiritual element. Many persons of faith lack depth and prophetic clarity because their devotional lives are superficial. Daily Bible study and journaling, undertaken with rigorous discipline, vitalizes my devotion to God. I do it first thing in the morning, just like I shave, shower, and dress for the day. If I don't practice this discipline, I find that it takes me only twenty-four hours to lose my fear of God.

What we do determines who we become. I want to see life through God's eyes and become passionate about the concerns that matter most to God, and this morning devotion helps me do that.

There is a big difference between deciding what I want to do and moving toward what God wants me to do. My devotional practice is the S.O.N. method that helps me see through the eyes of the SON of God. It involves the Scripture I read for the day, the Observations I journal as I read, and the practical applications I Name for my life. I then take time to express my feelings and thoughts in a written prayer. I'll show you a specific example of what I do when we explore the importance of devotion more in chapter 2.

Readiness

R represents readiness for lifelong learning. This is the intellectual element. I'm an avid reader, spending at least an hour a day studying the best practices of today's leadership culture while staying faithful to ancient truths. As a disciple of Jesus (the word *disciple* means "learner"), I want everything I read and observe to influence the faithfulness and effectiveness of my life ascent. Jesus said, "My sheep hear my voice" (John 10:27 KJV), and I want to learn to better recognize his voice.

What are you reading and learning? Many people stop learning once they've received a diploma. That's one reason people lose their effectiveness and relevance in their communities of worship or their workplaces. They simply quit learning. They have grown redundant and boring, having nothing new to say or offer. Any of us can grow similarly stale unless we remain committed to expanding our horizons, and that is exactly what this discipline is designed to accomplish.

In chapter 3 we will look at the importance of nurturing this disciplined practice of lifelong learning, and I'll share with you my personal daily regimen.

Investing

I denotes investing in key relationships, beginning with my family. This is the interpersonal element. I've rearranged my work schedule so that my life partner, Carolyn, feels supported by me rather than widowed by the church. I'm committed to putting my family before my work and church.

I also invest in other people who are strategic for the mission. All people are equally important to God, but not all are equally strategic when it comes to the expenditure of your time for God's purpose. Maybe for you it's a key group of volunteers who act as unpaid staff, or a few certain young people in need of a strong mentor. For me, it's the senior management team at Ginghamsburg Church. They are my "mission critical people," the only people besides my family who can contact me anytime, even when I'm on vacation.

> **All people are equally important to God, but not all are equally strategic for the expenditure of your time for God's purpose.**

Who is most strategic in *your* life? It's easy to let others set and fill my schedule based solely on who calls and says, "Pastor, I've got to see you today," but practicing this discipline helps me keep first things—and first people—first.

<u>V</u>ision

V indicates a vision for the future. This is the missional element. This is the most critical discipline, the one that all the others point toward and support, because no amount of learning, personal relationships, spiritual discipline, or physical health can give you momentum for life if your life has no purpose. If you have no future pictures, you'll live in the past. Your actions will be random, your movements aimless. It's critical that you have a vision, because you become your life picture, as my book *UnLearning Church* (new edition forthcoming in 2008 from Abingdon Press), emphasizes. At Ginghamsburg Church one of our current pictures is to create a twenty-six-acre campus with forty-eight living units for at-risk children. It will be an interracial, intergenerational community of foster parents and senior adults who will receive reduced-rate housing for mentoring the children.

As the book of Jeremiah opens, the Lord asks the prophet twice, "What do you see?" (Jer. 1:11, 13). It's important to see and develop the picture God has given you. You can't live someone else's picture. You have a unique calling; you must become who God has created *you* to be.

One characteristic of risk-takers and innovators is that they have clear faith-pictures of life. Like Joshua, they need courage to step into their dreams (see Josh. 1:1-9). Like Jeremiah, they must act upon everything God has commanded them or they will yield to fear. I worry about twenty-something church leaders who have great potential and yet begin to yield to the mean-spirited negativity of the congregation's godmothers and godfathers (my terms for those older members who don't want to see "their church" grow and change). They begin to relinquish their dreams to fear, and then they downsize God's vision.

<u>E</u>ating and <u>E</u>xercise

E stands for eating and exercise. This is the physical element. Sustaining momentum for life requires spiritual, social, and intellectual discipline, but you've got to make sure your body will be around for the future you've envisioned! With the Apostle Paul, I want to say, "Do as I do" in all areas of my life (see 1 Cor. 11:1), including the way I take care of my heart and health. I've already told you about my heart scare in 2000. Since then, I have become much more disciplined about my physical health. I run regularly, work out with weights, and watch my fats, carbs, and sugars. As a result I have more energy now in my fifties than I had in my thirties. I've come a long way since that night I collapsed at the dinner table.

Our church is United Methodist and belongs to the West Ohio Conference, which represents almost thirteen hundred pastors. In recent years, we have spent more money on health care for clergy than on mission. That is a painful reality. Our district superintendent sends out pedometers, asking each clergyperson to walk ten thousand steps a day. Our churches are filled with obese people who got that way simply through poor eating and inadequate exercise. That's both pulpit and pew. Obesity is a leading cause of preventable death in America, with deaths attributed to this disease numbering hundreds of thousands a year. I don't want to add to that total, and I've come to realize that, as part of my daily D-R-I-V-E regimen, eating and exercising are as spiritual as they are physical.

Model for Living

Faith + discipline = momentum for life.

The acronym D-R-I-V-E has become my way of life. Romans 12:1 says, "To offer your bodies as a living sacrifice, holy and pleasing to God—this is true worship." These are the disciplines that help me grow, with all of them contributing to my whole-life relationship with Jesus Christ. The equation is simple: faith + discipline = momentum for life.

What's your model for living? What foundation are you laying that will enable you to thrive when you hit resistance? Many Christians don't have an action plan for a well-balanced life. If you don't have a self-leadership model that works for you, I challenge you to test and explore this one.

Momentum Busters

To go where God is calling in your life and vocation, you must deal with the momentum busters of rationalization ("I make myself the exception"), procrastination ("I don't know where to start"), and the lack of visualization ("I don't have a picture of where I am going"). Any of these attitudes can prevent you from moving toward the purpose for which God has created you.

Rationalization: "I Make Myself the Exception"

Jerusalem is nicknamed "the city set on a hill" for good reason. It is poetically called "the city of our God . . . beautiful in elevation . . . the joy of all the earth" (Ps. 48:1-2 NRSV).

My wife and I once stayed in Jerusalem in January. The city is situated on an uneven rocky plateau at an elevation of some twenty-five hundred feet, and the temperature was hovering around thirty degrees Fahrenheit. Yet, a half hour later, only fourteen miles away at the Dead Sea, the lowest place on earth, the temperature was forty degrees higher. The elevation from Jerusalem to the Dead Sea drops by 3,800 feet, to 1,300 feet below sea level!

In ancient times, every faithful Jew (Israelite) was expected to make the pilgrimage to Jerusalem at least once a year. The place of worship at the top of the temple mount is the site God had designated for people to make an honorable, excellent offering. The temple was, in fact, the *only* place to do so. If you want to make an excellent offering to God, you can't stay on the plain; you must move up the mountain!

No matter where you came from, you faced quite a climb to reach the temple, the holy place of God. It was not a morning stroll, but an intense journey that took mental preparation and rigorous physical effort. This journey involved the pilgrim's full commitment of body, mind, and spirit.

Worshipers, while making the ascent to the Holy City, sang what are called the Psalms of Ascent. These songs are about reinforcing character, faith, and persistence in the face of resistance. We find them in the Bible today as Psalms 120 through 134.

God teaches us through these psalms that faith is a journey of ascent. One of our obstacles to life momentum is rationalization—telling our-

> **Faith is a journey of ascent. Our danger is rationalization, telling ourselves that we can live at the top without the effort of the climb.**

selves that we can live at the top without the effort of the climb. "I am the exception," we misguidedly tell ourselves. Some prominent professional athletes are discovering they can't cheat the effort of the climb with the assistance of performance-enhancing drugs without the consequence of diminished public respect and credibility.

I often run on a treadmill. I can do a speed of 7.4 miles per hour for half an hour with an incline of zero and have no problems. Sometimes I'll put the incline on one or two; I feel the difference, but I can still make it through the run. Once in a while at the gym someone who knows me will come by and press the "increase" button, moving the incline level up to ten. I feel it immediately as my heart rate increases and my body responds to the challenge.

God can be like the person punching the incline button, allowing the additional resistance to toughen us up. As God increases the incline of our path, our heart rate increases, which raises our passion, which fuels momentum. We grow through resistance. We learn to strive and thrive through resistance. The radical nature of the incline equips us with the momentum we need to ascend life's mountains. God gives us the strength to increase our life momentum by allowing resistance to come into our lives.

We learn to strive and thrive through resistance.

Nick Hoover, a twenty-seven-year-old from the Ginghamsburg Church community, participates in one of our three-times-a-week exercise classes. Nick says the feeling of being on a team has helped him deal with physical discipline as well as every other area of his life. He rises at 7:00 AM and makes it to the church gym for a 7:30 workout. "I feel like I'm on a team, training with accountability," he says. "I know if I miss, someone will ask me why I wasn't there." After two years, Nick has lost forty pounds and is a lot more energetic. He even ran his first official race. "Once you get going, it forms a habit," he says. "I feel better than I did in high school. I want to keep the momentum going. I don't want to regain the weight. I don't want to go back to the old Nick." He's not likely to go back if he keeps hanging out with others who have momentum.

I may be pleased with my physical condition but, like Nick, unless I work out I won't stay at my current level, much less gain ground. Followers of Jesus are called to "work out" our salvation knowing "it is God who works in you to will and to act in order to fulfill his good purpose" (Phil. 2:12-13). We're in a partnership with God that requires sweat equity on our part!

We're in a partnership with God that requires sweat equity on our part!

From Genesis to Revelation, we are called to a lifestyle of holiness—"without which no one will see the Lord" (Heb. 12:14 NRSV). Holiness is whole-life living. It means we are being transformed into God's likeness, that all areas of our lives reflect the One in whose image we were made.

Eternal life equals *quality* of life, where each part of me reflects the excellence of Christ's character. Many people think of eternal life only as *quantity* of life—being saved forever. Salvation is eternal, but if we don't participate with Christ in the life transformation of others and ourselves, then we won't have the quality of life that matches the excellence of Christ.

Psalm 122 uses an architectural comparison to illustrate the excellence of Christ as the harmonious order of God. Jerusalem is "built like a city / that is closely compacted together" (v. 3). Everything fits: stone upon stone, and row upon row. The psalmist looks forward to being in a place that represents the ultimate integrated wholeness of God: "I rejoiced with those who said to me, / 'Let us go to the house of the LORD' " (v. 1).

You don't just wake up one day and find yourself in a world as perfect as that represented by the psalmist. You need a momentum that will carry you all the way up the hill of eternity, where our offering to God is a lifestyle that reflects God's excellence.

Why We Rationalize

We live in a culture that has a passion for the immediate. We want the CliffsNotes version of God: happiness, success, and fulfilling relationships. We want "easy" and "now," and we try to make God work that way too. This cult of the instant has created an aversion to sweat. Avoiding perspiration at all costs, we lower the bar. We change God's standard of measure.

We turn to sex for sex's sake. "Why, God, did you create me with these urges?" we ask. Convincing ourselves that a loving God would never make life that hard, we lower the bar by having sex apart from the commitment to a lifelong, intimate relationship. Or we imagine ourselves having an affair with one of the "desperate housewives" on Wisteria Lane. I've heard that as many as one in four men struggle with addiction to Internet pornography—that's a lowered bar.[1]

Some have sold out by working for money rather than meaning, settling for a job rather than God's purpose. We buy bigger cars and more toys for our personal pleasure, forgetting that Jesus said, "The road is hard that leads to life" (Matt. 7:14 NRSV).

The call of Jesus is to journey on the narrow road. By lowering the bar, however, we arrogantly argue with what we read in the Bible, making ourselves exceptions to God's created moral order. We downplay Jesus' warning that "the gate is wide and the road is easy that leads to destruction, and there are many who take it" (Matt. 7:13 NRSV).

We rationalize, "That doesn't really mean me." Trouble is, we're not just to believe in Jesus but also to embrace the spirit and lifestyle of Jesus. The road is hard, and rationalizing in one area guarantees that we'll end up rationalizing in every area of life.

Some people see life's destination as making a lot of money and retiring in the Sunbelt, but that's a downsized goal! The destination of the Christ follower is not a retirement community of comfort, but a continual journey of ascent where God's purpose comes first. We are to seek first the kingdom of God (Matt. 6:33). We want to be wherever the reign of God is present.

> *Rationalizing in one area guarantees that we'll end up rationalizing in every area of life.*

Some of us have momentum in one area, but reach plateaus in others. You may be moving upward in your career while becoming stagnant in your marriage. I had momentum in ministry, but lacked it in my relationship with my wife.

Some have it in both ministry and marriage, but not in their physical bodies. A friend, Len Sweet, asked me twelve years ago, "Mike, what's up with your weight?" I was rationalizing my acceptance of the typical American pound-and-a-half annual weight gain that had resulted in an out-of-shape forty-three-year-old. "Your weight doesn't reflect the excellence of God," he observed.

Too many Christians ignore and excuse our sin of gluttony (Prov. 23:21). Remember, all leadership, all positive influence, begins with self-leadership. If I can't lead myself, I can't really lead anyone else—nor can you. Until your physical body experiences the momentum of ongoing care, you won't reach your full potential in influencing other people. A lowered bar of physical health affects the momentum of energy, spirit, and influence. Our bodies are the housing for the eternal God, vessels to contain the energy of God's powerful presence.

The same is true in the other areas we've discussed. They may not be as immediately visible, but they affect our ability to influence people in the right way just as much. I can feel the difference when I've neglected my devotional practices for just one day. If I were to give up my readiness to learn by abandoning my reading and study, it wouldn't be long before my mind began getting as soft as my belly had been. And I have no desire to return to the kind of marriage we had when my investment in my wife as a partner wasn't what it should have been. A well-rounded physical program works every area of the body in turn. A well-rounded approach to effective self-management concerns itself with every area of life. That's the kind of vision I want to strive for.

Proverbs 31 speaks of an amazing woman who is also a business entrepreneur and investor. Ever planning ahead, she teaches wisdom and kindness along the way. She's driven not by selfish achievement, but by a virtue that reaches far beyond her family. "She opens her arms to the poor / and extends her hands to the needy" (v. 20). The main emphasis is on her character, but notice that she "makes her arms strong" (v. 17 NRSV) and "she gets up while it is still night" (v. 15). She has physical stamina and conditioning as well. She reflects momentum in every area of D-R-I-V-E: **d**evotion to God, **r**eadiness for lifelong learning, **i**nvesting in key relationships, a **v**ision for the future, and **e**ating and exercise for physical strength.

Time to Repent

The opening words of the first Psalm of Ascent, sung at the beginning of the journey, are prayers of repentance. As they began their journey, worshipers sang, "I cry to the LORD . . . 'Deliver me, O LORD, / from lying lips, / from a deceitful tongue' " (Ps. 120:1-2 NRSV). In other words, "Deliver me from my rationalization and compromise."

What have I been rationalizing that isn't reflecting the excellence of God? I can name several areas. What about you? What rationalized, sweat-avoiding habits can you name that you must deal with? Get busy "working out" your salvation.

Procrastination: "I Don't Know Where to Start"

Procrastination is another huge momentum buster. In fact, failure comes in direct proportion to procrastination.

Have you ever gone into a test unprepared? If so, you may have experienced the feelings of inadequacy and self-doubt that procrastination, or the failure to take adequate measures of preparation, feeds. You've probably had the dream about a critical exam for which you failed to study, a play for which you hadn't memorized the lines, or an important presentation where you were embarrassed to discover yourself standing alone in your underwear. Procrastination comes back to haunt you in your dreams. It attaches itself to your psyche and continues to raise its ugly head through feelings of anxiety and dreams marked by panic, failure, and defeat.

Here's how it happens to me. I graduated from college thirty years ago, yet I still have this occasional recurring nightmare. I'm in class, it's exam day, and all quarter long I've forgotten about the course. I didn't show up even once. "I'm not going to graduate," I tell myself in great anxiety. Then I wake up—and I'm actually sweating. In real life, I know this is absurd. I graduated from college. I also have a master's degree and a doctorate! Yet look what deep roots developed from the seeds of my old habits of procrastination. They are so firmly rooted in my psyche that three decades later they can cause physical symptoms.

Procrastination is destructive, not just in terms of what we put off today but in how it attaches itself to the subconscious mind and begins to reproduce itself. "As he thinketh in his heart, so is he," says Proverbs 23:7 (KJV). Our inner, subconscious thoughts determine who and what we become.

Procrastination Leads to Poverty

The instructor in Proverbs asks, "How long will you lie there, O lazybones? / When will you rise from your sleep? / A little sleep, a little slumber, a little folding of the hands to rest, / and poverty will come upon you like a robber, / and want, like an armed warrior" (6:9-11 NRSV).

Procrastination always makes you poor. It leads to poverty not just in your wallet, as the writer of Proverbs warns, but in your spirit as well.

During one season of my life I was experiencing success in ministry, yet my marriage was poverty-stricken because I was trying to run it on autopilot. There were things I knew I needed to do in my marriage, but I was procrastinating—putting them off until another day. Most people do well in one area of their lives, though they experience poverty in others.

Compromise in any one area of my life will ultimately become an idolatrous cancer that will consume the rest.

Compromise in any one area of my life will ultimately become an idolatrous cancer that will consume the rest. Procrastination, failing to do today what shouldn't be put off until tomorrow, sows seeds of lifetime failure.

Set Apart for God

God calls us to a lifestyle of holiness. "Be holy," the Bible commands at least two dozen times. The term *holiness* may sound impractical or otherworldly to the modern ear, but it actually means "wholeness." When your life is set apart for God, when it is devoted to God's excellent purposes, it is made whole or complete. Perhaps holiness should be spelled as "wholiness." God is a God of whole-life excellence in every dimension, yet in our brokenness we rationalize and procrastinate about areas in our lives that are less than excellent.

In one of the early Psalms of Ascent, the worshipers make a commitment to go to God's prescribed place of promise, and they pledge to do so with a positive, proactive attitude. "I rejoiced with those who said to me, / 'Let us go to the house of the LORD.' . . . For the sake of the house of the LORD our God, / I will seek your prosperity" (Ps. 122:1, 9). I won't be content with anything less than the excellent purpose of God, seeking God's prosperity in every area of my life. Every area of my life needs to become an honorable, excellent offering to God.

What happens when you put off until tomorrow what you know you need to do today? What happens when you don't know how or where to start (or you do know and just plain don't want to do it!)? We find procrastination showing up in two ways.

1. Defaulting. We make a commitment to do what's right and to tackle the true priority, but at the last minute we default and do something less urgent or more comfortable.

To write this book, for instance, I made the commitment to stay home and work in my office on Tuesdays. I would have my coffee and devotion, run on my treadmill, shower, eat, and then dutifully open my computer. "OK, first paragraph, I'm ready for you to appear," I'd announce.

Actually, it wasn't as smooth as that. Before opening my computer, I'd sweat just thinking about what was ahead. When I was finally sitting in front of my computer, I'd ask the appropriate question regarding my priority for that day: "What's a good opening for this chapter?" But after all of twelve seconds of looking at a blank screen, I'd shift, telling myself, "Hmmm. Nothing jumping out at me. Maybe I'll check my e-mail." Somehow the less urgent matter would take over the morning. Suddenly it would be noon and I wouldn't have written anything for the book yet, although I'd have devised yet another angle of procrastination: "Well, half the day is gone, so I'll just wait until next Tuesday to start again."

"But you don't know my schedule," you protest. "I'm not putting things off; life is just too crazy right now for me to cover everything that needs to be done."

Many ancient worshipers never made the pilgrimage to the house of God because they felt overwhelmed by the preparations and hassles. In the winter it snows in Jerusalem, and in the summer it's hot. "It's not such a good day to go up to the house of the Lord," people would say as they procrastinated. In spring or fall, they might cite problems with the traffic, with feeling uncomfortable in crowds, with not having the right clothes, or with not knowing what to do with the kids. "It's easier to stay home," many people would conclude. But nothing worthwhile is easy, and the road to the house of God has always been narrow.

You've got to deal with your big "but"—the big procrastination statements you use on yourself. "But I don't have time to get close to God," or "but I don't have time to exercise because I'm too busy." What's *your* biggest "but"?

- D - If you're too busy to spend time talking to your Creator— that's what **devotion** actually is—then you're defaulting to lesser tasks.
- R - If the tyranny of the urgent squelches your **readiness** for lifelong learning, then you're defaulting to lesser tasks.
- I - If you don't have any room in your life to **invest** in key relationships, then you're defaulting to lesser tasks.
- V - If you're too consumed with the present to cultivate a **vision** of the future, then you're defaulting to lesser tasks.
- E - If you don't have time to **exercise** or **eat** right—you're not recognizing your body as the temple of God—then you're defaulting to lesser tasks.

2. Feeling Overwhelmed. Some people feel they have so much to do that they don't know where to start. The pile of ironing has stacked up for four weeks and you have only two clean shirts left—and even they require deodorant in unlikely places. You don't know where to start, so you go to the refrigerator and dig into some ice cream.

When you're feeling overwhelmed, you must do the first hard thing. In your house, it may mean doing fifteen minutes of ironing before you open the refrigerator again. In your spiritual house, it may mean taking a fifteen-minute walk around your block, putting all your cares onto God before you begin your task list. "Cast all your anxiety on him because he cares for you" (1 Pet. 5:7).

Good intentions or professions of belief are not the same thing as commitment. No matter how well intentioned, many people don't make the commitment to finish the journey. In faith development, altitude requires a journey of exertion. Make the commitment to do the first thing.

That First Worst Step

My wife and I have a giant schnauzer named Luka. He loves to be wherever we are. Whether we're cooking, watching television, or working out, Luka likes to hang out with us.

He has a little problem, though. We call it the procrastination shuffle. Suppose we're upstairs and we call him to join us. He'll put one paw on the bottom step, and then he'll pause. "Nope!" his brain signals. Then he pulls that paw back, puts the other paw on the first step, leans forward—and pauses again. Getting started is a real challenge for this 125-pound dog. We've watched him do his procrastination shuffle for as long as two minutes. (View Luka's procrastination shuffle at http://www.ginghamsburg.org/mflresources.) Finally he begins the climb. Once he gets started he's OK, but often he expends more energy taking that first step than climbing the entire staircase.

I'm like that too. When I get a feeling about something that I should be doing, how do I respond? Too often the biggest temptation is to take two aspirins and go to bed until the feeling goes away.

I'm not alone. There's even an official term for a speaker or author's procrastination dilemma: writer's block. Anne Lamott, one of my top-shelf authors, talks about getting herself started by writing "shitty" first drafts.[2] You have to make the commitment to start somewhere.

You have to make the commitment to start somewhere.

"Almost all good writing begins with terrible first efforts," says Anne Lamott in *Bird by Bird* (Anchor Books, 1994).[3] The title's metaphor came from her brother, who at ten years old was trying to write a report on birds. He'd had three months to write, and it was due the next day.

> He was at the kitchen table close to tears, surrounded by binder paper and pencils and unopened books on birds, immobilized by the hugeness of the task ahead. Then my father [an accomplished writer] sat down beside him, put his arm around my brother's shoulder, and said, "Bird by bird, buddy. Just take it bird by bird."[4]

Suppose I keep reading about the need to eat better, but I'm confused. Everyone is talking about exercise and eating, but I'm overwhelmed and don't know where or how to begin.

I tried to start a fitness program on my own. I did five jumping jacks and started to sweat, so I figured I had gotten my heart going adequately for that day. I tried a few push-ups. Going down was OK, but I had a lot of trouble pushing back up. Running was extremely uncomfortable. Actually, it seemed impossible. Too many parts of me bounced as I ran!

Not knowing where to start or change, I had zero momentum. I felt overwhelmed, and so I quit. I tried it another day, another week, and another month—and I quit each time, long before I had any momentum to show for my good intentions. I couldn't lead myself past where I was. Nor can you.

My breakthrough came when I decided that I needed someone ahead of me, someone experiencing success that could get me unstuck. I needed a coach. I asked for a trainer.

I found Chastity Layne Slone, a certified personal trainer from our Ginghamsburg Church family. She asked how well I could run, and she tested me with a moderate run around our hundred-acre church campus. After running for what felt like ten minutes, I began to complain. "We've got to stop and walk," I moaned. Unfortunately, I had gone only one minute, twenty-eight seconds according to Chastity's stopwatch! She wouldn't let me stop, saying, "If you stop, it's almost impossible to get going again." This is the essence of momentum. Stop and it's almost impossible to get going again.

The essence of momentum: If you stop, it's almost impossible to get going again.

For lasting momentum, you need the accountability of a person who is ahead of you, someone who has demonstrated success, accomplishment, and faithfulness in the area in which you are struggling. This is where the church plays a powerful role. Our church is using a life-coach model, providing classes in everything from fitness to finances. If you commit to do the first hard thing, we'll commit to help you get there. We want your whole life—body, soul, and spirit—to become an honorable, excellent offering to God.

Many people at Ginghamsburg Church are doing a *Transformation Journal*,[5] a daily Scripture journal designed to take us deeper in devotion to God. Every Wednesday night we have a life coach, Pastor Mike Bowie, teach on the *Journal* Scriptures, taking people to the next level of growth.

We offer classes in a wide variety of areas where people typically get stuck. We know that all of us need coaches who are ahead of us. Just as important, we know that at some point each of us is acting as an example, a coach, even if we're not aware of it.

Poor Visualization: "I Don't Have a Picture of Where I Am Going"

The Bible says, "Where there is no vision, the people perish" (Prov. 29:18 KJV). To have vision is to have the ability to see with eyes of faith. Vision knows how to articulate God's promising possibilities for the future.

The Psalms of Ascent are a constant reminder to see, from God's perspective, both the world and our own purpose in it. As the ascent becomes steeper, we need a clear reminder of why we started the climb in the first place.

As the ascent becomes steeper, we need a clear reminder of why we started the climb in the first place.

With the ancient pilgrims, we call on God because we need help: "I call on the LORD in my distress, / and he answers me" (Ps. 120:1). We want to see life from the perspective of heaven: "I lift up my eyes to you, / to you who sit enthroned in heaven" (Ps. 123:1). As dangers and temptations lurk around the perilous bend, we need to hang on to the vivid picture of our destination.

As with most spiritual principles, the examples in our own lives can be mundane. They can be as simple as the clutter around us. We let up on discipline just enough to allow cluttered spaces in our lives. They lead quickly to cluttered thinking, which translates to a cluttered spirit and an undisciplined lifestyle. Allow a space to become undisciplined or disorganized and it grows and begins to take on a life of its own.

A few years ago Carolyn's mom moved into a retirement center. Carolyn spent a week sorting through her mother's possessions. It was hard for her to give or throw away any of it—so many items had a specific meaning or special memory. Where could she put all the stuff? Our garage was the solution.

We built our own house in 1993, and we've always worked hard to keep our garage clean. It was part of our unspoken vision to avoid clutter, both literally and metaphorically. Our two cars always fit nicely inside. But with the loads of furniture, boxes, and knickknacks, our garage was full!

Then our son Jonathan came home from college. Our standard house rule had always been that anyone coming home from an extended time away had to carry everything inside to his or her room or to the storage room in the basement. But this time Jonathan didn't do all that. He didn't even ask to change the plan. He now saw the garage as a place of disorganization and simply added all his college stuff to our growing monster in the garage!

Is your home or apartment like that? When you allow space for clutter, the pile somehow grows. This same idea works in the rest of your life. If you allow clutter in your spiritual life, marriage, finances, or anywhere else, it will grow. More clutter will accumulate along the way. Soon you'll have a monster in your life.

At some point, the vision of a clean, well-ordered space disappears. We lose sight of the initial plan. And where there

If you allow clutter in your spiritual life, marriage, finances, or anywhere else, it will grow.

is no vision, there is no road map for change. We get mired in the problem.

Much of Jonathan's stuff, like yours or mine, had special sentimental value. As an avid baseball player, he owned fifty broken bats. Each bat had a meaning, just like all the items in Carolyn's pile. Still, one holiday weekend, I told Jonathan he had to clean out his stuff.

For us, the vision was that clean, clear, usable garage. The road map was a boxful of garbage bags begging to be filled. The primary path we selected went from the garage to a trash pile on the curb. Because we nurtured the vision, because we attached a road map to it, the plan worked. I can now put two vehicles (and one motorcycle!) back into our garage.

God is a God of order!

The metaphor used in Psalm 122:3 is based on the dwelling of God, which is well designed and strategically built. "Jerusalem is built like a city / that is closely compacted together."

Architects begin by designing blueprints—life maps, or visions put to paper. Strategic lives likewise develop from well-designed blueprints. They work out of disciplined plans. You need a life map, a critical plan with a definite starting point. What's your life map to holiness—to wholeness? Where are you making a less-than-honorable offering to God?

The pilgrims who were on ascent visualized standing inside the gates of Jerusalem long before they ever arrived: "Our feet are standing in your gates, Jerusalem" (Ps. 122:2). Vision creates momentum that is self-sustaining and self-fulfilling.

One of the five life practices for balance and self-leadership in D-R-I-V-E is the practice of visualization. Chapter 5 ("Visioning for the Future") will focus on seeing ahead through eyes of faith.

The momentum of God's purpose and dream is too great for any of us not to reflect the excellent character of God in any area of our lives. The Christian has made a commitment to a lifetime journey of faith. Following Jesus is hard. We are to go where Jesus is going, to be who Jesus is being, and to do what Jesus is doing.

The Bible says to work out your salvation—that means a commitment to sweat! The great evangelist Dwight L. Moody said, "We pray like it is all up to God. We work like it is all up to us." Grace is not passive. Grace is active: Our sweat meets Jesus' blood, and that's where the miracle takes place.

The Apostle Paul says, "Straining toward what is ahead, I press on toward the goal to win the prize for which God has called me heavenward in Christ Jesus" (Phil. 3:13-14 NIV).

Today is the day of salvation. Today is the day your sweat needs to meet Jesus' blood.

Opportunity is not going to come along and drag you off the couch. You have to put yourself out there. Only you can make the commitment to start the climb.

What hard thing will you tackle first? Deal with your big "but" and take action today!

"Now is the time of God's favor, now is the day of salvation" (2 Cor. 6:2). Enter into God's fullness and wholeness.

> **Only you can make the commitment to start the climb.**

Sustaining Momentum

This book is a five-part journey of ascent. Each of the following chapters introduces a daily life discipline around the acronym of D-R-I-V-E. These five life practices will enable you to build and sustain momentum to make your life an honorable, excellent offering and to reach God's promised destination.

Devotion: Begin each day with the practice of Bible study, meditation, journaling, and prayer.

Readiness for lifelong learning: Live like a child in school, no matter what your chronological age. Take some time each day for the purpose of growing in "life science." Become a student of the culture, so you can continue to make a meaningful contribution in God's world.

Investing in key relationships: Many leaders have fallen here. This is the everyday practice of keeping your heart in the home first and then investing in those people who are most strategic to the mission that God has called you to.

Vision for the future: Look forward through eyes of faith. Articulate with clarity God's preferred future; make daily strategic corrections to your life picture.

Eating and exercise: Take small steps and then bigger ones, exercising your "push back" muscle at the next meal (pushing yourself back from the table) to go take a vigorous walk. Take care of your body for the long haul and find more energy for today.

These five activities are designed to reach God's purpose in your life and mine.

Before You Begin the Next Chapter

In what area are you not doing so well? Where are you stuck?

Pause to name the specific momentum buster that you want to break through. It may be a favorite rationalization, a habit of procrastination, or an unhealthy picture of your future. Write a prayer of repentance, naming the specific area you want to work on in God's grace, making a commitment to cooperate with God in breaking this barrier.

Direct your prayer around Psalm 120:2.

> Deliver me, O Lord, from lying lips and a deceitful tongue. Save me from rationalization, procrastination, and a lack of visualizing your bigger purpose for my life mission. By faith I enter into your salvation from _____ [name of specific sin]. By faith I will work out my salvation by _____ [make commitment to a new discipline outlined in this book]. I welcome and invite the Holy Spirit's work in my life because of what Jesus did on the cross for me. Amen.

As you begin this climb, this journey of ascent, who can go with you? Who can hold you up in prayer? How can you help support someone else? Why not read this book with an accountability partner or in a group? You could cover the next five chapters as a five-week journey of discipline. Each chapter will offer a series of short questions, such as the ones listed on the following page. Your group can help hold you accountable by talking about what you learn as you go through each chapter.

Rest Area Reflections

Read aloud the main Scripture, Psalm 122.

1. Conversions are moments when we experience a major turnaround in our thinking or behavior. Can you name the time and place of your last conversion?

2. Think of a place in your life that does not fully reflect the excellence of God.

3. What is a healthy step you would love to take or need to take, but can't yet imagine taking?

4. Are you rationalizing (making excuses) or procrastinating (don't know how to start) instead of taking your next step on the journey of ascent?

5. A life map can help us keep a future picture. Consider drawing a map of your own life and where you hear/see God leading you. What is up ahead on your map?

CHAPTER TWO

devotion to God

DEVOTION> *Focused commitment of time and energy;
dedication; faithfulness; deep affection.*

PASSION> *Intensity; strong emotion; ardor; zeal;
motivation.*

*Very early in the morning, while it was still dark, Jesus got
up, left the house and went off to a solitary place, where he
prayed. (Mark 1:35)*

Devotion and passion are powerful motivators, twin emotions that create the energy of momentum in our lives. Many anointed leaders of God have discovered that passion is a greater persuasive force than cognitive belief in determining life direction and behavior.

King David was one such anointed leader. He had experienced the hand of God working through his life in powerful ways, helping him become the greatest king Israel ever knew. God had called him for a formidable purpose—to lead a unified nation that honored and served God, one that valued justice, prosperity, and peace. He was known as a man of great faith and confident passion. "In your strength I can crush an army; / with my God I can scale any wall" (2 Sam. 22:30 NLT).

David was a man after God's heart (1 Sam. 13:14, Acts 13:22), fervent about everything he did, from battling Goliath the God-mocker to planning the great temple. David's passionate heart, however, also succumbed to less honorable endeavors. Following his own pleasures, he became obsessed with another man's wife, and then compounded his affair with murder. David's failure was a result not of his cognitive belief but of his unbridled passion.

In a similar way, Satan's attack on Jesus in the wilderness was directed not toward Jesus' beliefs but toward his human passions. "After fasting forty days and forty nights, [Jesus] was hungry. The tempter came to him

and said, 'If you are the Son of God, tell these stones to become bread' "
(Matt. 4:2-3). Satan tempted Jesus to shift the focus of his devotion away
from his Father to food and fame. Evil went directly for the jugular vein
of Jesus' human passions rather than simply trying to appeal to his cognitive beliefs.

The Smell of Passion

Your devotion reveals what you care about, pointing toward the focus
of your deepest desires. People can sense your devotion. They can *smell*
your passions. Belief, by contrast, is something you must describe verbally.

My leadership at Ginghamsburg Church has been on an upward ascent
for more than a quarter of a century, yet no one knows my political
beliefs. I have never shared my political persuasions in a message or
allowed partisan issues to be the focus of my ministry.

One weekend I asked my congregation to tell me what I am passionate
about. I was expecting them to respond, "Jesus!" but instead they shouted
back with one voice, "BASEBALL!" They don't know my political views,
but they can smell my passion. I am indeed a baseball enthusiast, but until
that moment I didn't know it was that noticeable. I thought about how
they responded. If baseball comes across as a greater passion in my life
than God, then I need to realign my heart.

The same principle works at home. Our children pick up on our passion far more than they hear our words. Their views and values are more
influenced by the objects of our devotion than by our stated beliefs. Is it
any wonder that they readily adopt our zeal for music, money, movies, or
athletics while struggling to articulate our beliefs and tuning out our religious traditions after they leave home?

Devotion reflects ultimate values. Devotion reveals true belief. Your
greatest enthusiasm betrays your true object
of worship.

Likewise, motivation can be boiled down to
passion. Your passions, more than your beliefs,
determine your life actions and directions.

Anyone who struggles with discipline or
addictive behaviors understands the power of
passion. Have you ever gone to a restaurant
determined to pass on dessert, only to be
derailed when the server told you about the triple-chocolate cheesecake?

> **Your greatest enthusiasm betrays your true object of worship.**

28

Your beliefs tell you that you don't need the high-cholesterol fat calories, but your appetite overrules those beliefs. The servers are trained to know that your passions will prove stronger than your beliefs.

Most people think, "If only I could increase my belief in God, things would be different." Most likely it is not your *belief* in God that needs to increase; it is your *passion* for God that must grow in order to give you the momentum to thrive in the face of resistance.

Devotion is stronger than structures of intellectual belief. Devotion reflects what you ultimately care about, what you value. If you're ever in doubt as to what that is, just ask those who know you best what your passions are and they will tell you immediately. Whatever you value most highly becomes the object of your worship, and what you worship *drives* you! We don't need to increase our belief in God—we need to increase our passion for God!

Present to God's Presence

I have found that it takes me about twenty-four hours to lose a healthy fear of God. When that happens, my heart turns its attention to counterfeit gods. This is why I must begin each day with the lifelong discipline of devotion.

When I come home from work, I enter the house through the garage, pass through the laundry room, and come into an eat-in kitchen that Carolyn and I both enjoy. It has a desk where we put the mail for each other to see, and I find it relaxing to thumb through the day's envelopes when I first come home.

One evening, Carolyn was excited to tell me something, but my first impulse was to check the mail. Carolyn was chatting away about her day, but I was distracted. Partway through the discussion she said, "Wait a minute! I'm talking and you're not here!"

In the same way, God is always speaking, but we're not always present to the relationship. Does it ever seem to you that God is hiding? The real problem is that *we* are not aware of God's presence.

Devotion is time focused on God's presence. Because it can be hard work, it requires intentional discipline. My God-stalking efforts involve Bible study, meditation on what I'm reading, prayer, and journaling—using our church's *Transformation Journal* and the S.O.N. method of daily devotion. As I have outlined, that method involves Scripture reading,

Devotion is time focused on God's presence.

<u>O</u>bservation, and <u>N</u>aming the personal princi-ple that relates to my life in the present. These practices create in me an awareness of the presence of God, allowing the personal voice of God to speak to my life situation and me each day.

A More Passionate Life Focus

The daily practice of devotion, of being fully present to God's presence, continually renews a healthy, passionate life focus. Psalm 121, the second Psalm of Ascent, begins, "I lift up my eyes to the mountains—where does my help come from?" The phrase *my help* refers to my meaning, my purpose, and my life-empowerment. Metaphorically speaking, this journey of ascent is to the house of God, the place of God's ultimate purpose and presence in my life.

Many of us read these verses and envision nature in its pristine beauty. A colorful hillside or mountainous setting is a place of inspiration and awe for many. Indeed, I love North Carolina's mountains. Each time I visit them, I get in touch with creation, and I see God's thumbprint.

For the Israelite pilgrims who sang this psalm on the way up to Jerusalem's house of worship, however, the mountains held a different meaning. When these psalms were written, the hills contained shrines and altars to pagan gods, counterfeits of the real thing. These subtle sirens tempted travelers to stop short of the ultimate objective, to dabble in their destructive influences. Pilgrims could be led astray by many brands of over-the-counter gods offering instant remedies for every traveling need. Worried about the stock market? The gods of fertility would guarantee the success of your produce. Fatigued by the heat? You could go to the sun priest and pray for protection from the elements. Suffering from emotional distress? The moon goddess could remove such pain for a small fee. Love-starved or driven by lust? Sacred prostitutes, male and female, were available to relieve your sexual tension. The red-light districts and porno chat rooms of today are nothing new. The great temptation for any child of God is to stop short of true transformation and seek mere relief.

I have been on a God-journey for thirtysome years. Life has at times become tiring and it often feels difficult. Where do I find relief? The temptation is to look to the hills around me for some kind of immediate gratification. It would be easy enough simply to turn off the road on my way up the path to Jerusalem and the house of God.

Many of these same influences pervade our culture as well, bombarding us with incessant advertisements for over-the-counter gods, fast-food substitutes, and feel-good potions designed to help us avoid the strenuous climb of life. Many on the path of ascent have turned aside toward the sounds of the lustful sirens. One leader from a conservative denomination told me that approximately one third of the pastors in his district who were disciplined or removed from ministry lost their positions because of sexual immorality or addiction to Internet pornography.

There are many gods of immediacy along the road making false claims, offering CliffsNotes versions of fulfillment, happiness, and meaning. You can purchase spells that will protect you from ills and spills or provide thrills to distract you from the perils of the road. As you ascend the road of God's calling, the voices from the hills grow louder in their attempts to lure you to the cultural shrines that promise immediate relief and self-gratification.

> **As you ascend the road of God's calling, the voices grow louder in their attempts to lure you to promises of self-gratification.**

Danger Zone

During this last half of my life I am setting aside a few days several times a year to meet with small groups of pastors in living room or retreat environments. It's one thing to mentor from a platform, speaking to hundreds or thousands at a conference, but what I really want to do at this stage of my ministry is sit down on a couch and challenge young pastors face-to-face not to compromise in their own Psalms of Ascent.

Not long ago I met with two dozen young leaders, challenging them to be everything God created them to be. We held our pastor's practicum in Ginghamsburg's original 1876 church building on our south campus. Sitting in a comfortable chair, propping my feet on an end table, I reminded them that all leadership begins with self-leadership. "You can't lead anyone farther than you're leading yourself," I explained. I told them about my acronym of D-R-I-V-E. "Before you can ever lead anybody else you have to be able to lead yourself, and it begins right here in these five daily disciplines."

One pastor had apparently been eyeing my boots as he listened to me share. At the first break of the morning he approached me and said, "Do you just wear those boots or do you really have a bike?" He had recognized my footwear as Harley-Davidson boots.

"I'm getting a bike next month," I answered with a big smile. It would be my first Harley. I'd spent sixteen years saving for it because of our family commitment to live debt-free and not to divert money earmarked for mission. God had used my delayed gratification to build character, but I was eager for my bike's delivery date and had already purchased my riding boots. I was breaking them in that day. This young pastor was the proud owner of a Harley, and he knew the power of the boots and the lure of the bike. For both of us, and many other people, the Harley is not just a mode of transportation—it's a passion!

The danger is that our passions tend to take on lives of their own. The hillside shrines call to me as I move into the section of the path marked "midlife crisis." I shouldn't be surprised when those hillside shrines along the road of ascent distract my eyes. Passions tempt us, saying, "Hey, it's not hard! Come over here and I will give you life!" Harley-Davidson has worked hard to create a cultlike subculture with its life-offering promises. The company's slogan is "Live to Ride, Ride to Live," and I find myself anxious to buy the leathers, ride, and find my life's passion.

> **The danger is that our passions tend to take on lives of their own.**

Danger zone! "Do not turn to idols or make metal gods for yourselves," Leviticus 19:4 states. "I am the LORD your God." Along with many others, I can easily be tempted toward idolatry, showing greater passion for metal than for God. I have been on this journey for a long time, and I need to be conscious of where my relief comes from. As I've said, it takes me about twenty-four hours to lose my focus on God. That's why the first discipline of each morning involves an intense practice of being fully present to God's presence. I am then reminded, "Surely the [idolatrous] commotion on the hills / and mountains is a deception; / surely in the LORD our God is the salvation of Israel" (Jer. 3:23). I remember that my help is not found in the promised relief of the hills but that "my help comes from the LORD, / the Maker of heaven and earth" (Ps. 121:2).

Wrestling Match

I am drawn to the story of Jacob in Genesis 32. Jacob was going through some kind of peril on life's journey. He was literally in the midst of a process of ascent, and all night long he wrestled with God, who had come to him in physical form. God said to Jacob, "Let me go!" and Jacob replied, "I am not going to let you go until you bless me."

Wrestling with God means not just slipping into church on Sunday, then going back home and automatically enjoying God's blessing. God doesn't respond to the "really quick, bottom line, right now, here I am" method of devotion. It's all about the relationship. I have been in this relationship with God thirty-plus years, and intimacy in any relationship is hard work. It's an everyday kind of discipline, and I must be willing to hang on to God, to work until resolution and connection emerge. If I let go of God too soon, I am done!

As with Jacob, a residual limp reminds me of my daily dependence. Anyone who has wrestled in school knows that wrestling is a hot, sweaty, uncomfortable discipline. Miracles are not magic. Anything worthwhile in life comes from a sustained momentum in the same direction.[1] There is nothing quick about leaving a legacy. There's nothing easy about mining the true meaning out of our existence.

Anything worthwhile in life comes from a sustained momentum in the same direction.

Jacob discovered that the God of his ancestors is not to be manipulated for selfish purposes or for instant relief and gratification. Simple Sunday school solutions will not suffice in the ascent through the fog of the world as we know it. These quick remedies offer the illusion of spiritual meaning while denying real truth. Jacob grabbed hold of God and refused to let go. "I will not . . . I cannot . . . I must not let go until I live in your (w)holiness!"

In Oprah Winfrey's O magazine, I read about a woman trying to find answers for life in Buddhism. She began, "The God of my childhood is not what I am after. What I am seeking is a rugged, everyday type of deity—one that can provide a compassionate lens through which to view my life, a split-second of serenity between the moment the milk gets spilled on my new cashmere sweater and my reaction. I need a spiritual practice, if only to comfort myself that while I am clearly getting older, I'm doing my level best to get wiser, too."[2]

God-wrestling is an everyday practice. It is through this daily wrestling that God imparts the compassion and serenity the woman mentioned above craves so deeply. Any wrestler or athlete understands the discipline and energy required to be fit for a match. Likewise, every day I need to be disciplined in my devotion to Jesus. I am constantly tempted to use Jesus' name but to live out of the soft, secular worldview that is so predominant in the culture of our churches.

Many people in the church do the same thing. They name Jesus' name but still trust materialism to provide meaning and security. This is why most of us merely donate to God. When you make a donation, you don't alter your lifestyle; it doesn't cost you anything.

> **When you make a donation, you don't alter your lifestyle; it doesn't cost you anything.**

Jesus calls us to sacrifice, to go the way of the cross. Sacrifice involves willfully altering your lifestyle to achieve a higher, greater purpose. Every day I must wrestle with God to remind me of the why and the Who of my life. This practice of devotion, my 6:00 AM wrestling match, renews my life focus, and if I let go of God too soon, I am done.

The Jesus Movement

One of the most incredible changes I've seen in my years of ministry has been the marginalization of Christian influence in Western civilization.

Some may remember the Jesus movement of the 1970s. I was part of it. Growing up, I related much more to rock music than to the Christian liturgy of my childhood. Then, in the 1970s, Campus Crusade for Christ at the University of Cincinnati had a powerful impact on my life. Our meetings often had the raw, living-room atmosphere of a countercultural movement.

I wasn't alone in my newfound faith. It seemed everyone was talking about Jesus—former Dallas Cowboy star Roger Staubach, President Jimmy Carter, even several beauty queens who won the Miss America pageant. A number of other prominent people looked into Christianity, including musician Bob Dylan in his album *Slow Train Coming*. Even the *Tonight Show* bandleader Doc Severinsen was converted for a season!

With so much conversation about Jesus, many of us thought we were on the verge of a global spiritual awakening. We naively thought that if Jesus had radically changed our lives, we could place Jesus within others' cultural contexts and their lives could be radically changed as well. Although this era had all the earmarks of a Jesus revolution, we compromised the true values of the kingdom of God. We traded the revolution for the relevance of secular culture.

Consequently, the church of the twenty-first century struggles with spiritual impotency. Researcher George Barna reminds us that 95 percent of the people in church never bring another person with them. More powerfully, he finds that while 120 million attend church on a regular basis, only fifteen million—less than 10 percent—define success in terms of spiritual development.[3]

A Jesus Worldview

I must continually challenge my worldview with the worldview of Jesus. A worldview is a set of fundamental beliefs that determines your primary life values, decisions, and actions. Your worldview has more to do with your values than your religion. It sets the course of your life action. A worldview determines everything from your sexual mores to your political persuasions.

> **Your worldview has more to do with your values than your religion.**

Tim Keller, who is lead pastor at Redeemer Presbyterian Church in New York City (www.redeemer.com), has good insight on the types of worldviews found in North American churches today. Redeemer's vision is to renew New York City socially, spiritually, and culturally. Tim talks about the diversity of worldviews in American culture, and I am synthesizing these into four predominant worldviews found in the institutional church today—the secular, the soft-secular, the postsecular, and, finally, the worldview of Jesus.

1. Secular. People with a secular worldview are skeptical of anything supernatural. They may or may not believe in some sort of higher power, but they live their lives within the confines of human logic. They make clear distinctions between secular and sacred. They believe that to involve faith in the daily marketplace of life is tantamount to superstition. They see belief in a supernatural God as a barrier to social progress. Theirs is a humanistic point of view with the basic premise that human beings have a universal need to create their own meaning, values, and destiny. They view the world solely in materialistic terms, convinced that nothing exists outside of matter—the molecules that make up people and things. People and things are the only resources available to solve all the problems of life.

You'll find relatively few people with this mind-set attending church regularly. Most secular people in North America are Caucasian, over the age of forty, and from Protestant-Catholic-Jewish backgrounds. They run many of the elite universities in North America that were originally focused on educating people for ministry, including Harvard and Yale, and many others that have separated (either officially or unofficially) from the denominations that founded them. For example, more than one hundred colleges and universities are United Methodist affiliated. Most were "designed for evangelism" but have been "swept up . . . into the culture and purposes of the American academy," according to *The Dying of the Light: The Disengagement of Colleges and Universities from Their Christian Churches*.[4] It cites as representative one university chaplain, a United Methodist cleric, who describes his responsibility, as he sees it, to "defend the importance of the university as a secular culture against all forms of orthodoxy."[5]

2. Soft-secular. The predominant worldview in churches is "soft-secular." People with a soft-secular worldview believe in God and claim a faith identity, but God is not their first priority or passion. They live comfortably in two spheres, sacred and secular, but when pressed for time their default always goes to the secular. They bring Jesus into their worldview instead of being converted into his. Soft-secular people may confess Jesus but trust the values of secular culture, putting their faith in material possessions to provide meaning rather than trusting God's promise of provision. They make religious donations rather than life sacrifices. It is difficult for soft-secular people to make significant time or financial commitments to their churches.

People with a soft-secular mind-set tend to be over the age of forty. They represent the predominant worldview in baby-boomer churches.

> **Soft-secular people may confess Jesus, but trust the values of secular culture.**

3. Post-secular. A third worldview is more widespread in people under the age of forty. It's found in what some call millennial churches or Gen X churches. Post-secular people are open to the supernatural but biased toward an expressive individualism that leads to relativism. "It's true if it works for me," they believe. Those who view life this way are centered in today. The present is all that matters, and anything in the past is irrelevant to the expression of self and truth. Likewise, commitments made today—such as the "I do" of marriage—are viewed as intentions that may or may not work for tomorrow or the future.

Many times I see post-secular people make what seem to be heartfelt commitments to Jesus, but when identification with Jesus means a missed opportunity for a relationship, a sexual encounter, or a professional advancement, they bail on the Christian commitment. Post-seculars attempt to fit Christ into their own worldview instead of being transformed into his, creating a cult of self. Sadly, this is the worldview of many in the church.

4. Christian. The fourth worldview found in the church today says that commitment to Christ is bigger than my life or my lifetime. Truth will work and prevail because it is true, but it may not prevail in my lifetime. In fact, living for truth may cost me my life.

Taking on the Worldview of Jesus

Jesus said, "For whoever wants to save their life will lose it, but whoever loses their life for me will save it" (Luke 9:24). Heeding his call that we deny ourselves and take up Jesus' cross daily (Luke 9:23) for the sake of the coming kingdom of God is the only way we can find life. This worldview flies in the face of the soft-secular mind-set found so widely in churches. Life is not about me but about me being a link in the chain of God's generations. It's not about my wants, my passions, or my needs, but it is about my commitment to God's greater purpose and the coming of the kingdom of God! The sacred trust I have from all generations is to connect the covenant of the past with the promised coming kingdom, knowing from Jesus' warning that pain may be part of the package. Obeying the truth may lead to ostracism, loss of relationship, persecution, and rejection in my lifetime. Obeying the truth of God may lead to smaller churches, like the small group of followers who were closest to Jesus. After all, his church consisted of only 120 people at the time of his death. Many of us would not consider this an indicator of ministry success. He would not have been asked to speak at a conference on the subject of "breaking the 200 barrier"! Perhaps we are working from a faulty measure of success, driven by the values of our culture and not the kingdom of God.

We need to rethink church and reimagine it from God's perspective. For a moment, imagine that the secular parts of our culture have no sway over you. Forget also what your boss, bishop, board of directors, or church polity book require of you. From Micah 6:8 take a reality check: "What does the LORD require of you? / To act justly and to love mercy / and to walk humbly with your God." Notice the verb in this passage: to *act*, not to *believe*. Likewise, the account of the early church is called the Acts of the Apostles, not the *beliefs* of the apostles. Not even the *intentions* of the apostles!

Isaiah 58 talks about a faith group that embodied a soft-secular view of spiritual renewal. They had been fasting, gathering for instruction, and praying—all the right things for all the wrong reasons. They did all the religious rituals, with none of the spiritual power. "Where are you, God?" they ask. God tells them, in essence, "I'm not interested in how many butts you put in chairs at your weekend services." Power with God is a result of our actions toward people. "Is not this the kind of fasting I have chosen: / to loose the chains of injustice / and untie the cords of the yoke, / to set the oppressed free / and break every yoke? / Is it not to share your food with the hungry / and to provide the poor wanderer with shelter?" (vv. 6-7).

This is not just an Old Testament issue. Jesus reiterated: "Whatever you did for one of the least of these brothers and sisters of mine, you did for me" (Matt. 25:40). To have Jesus' worldview is to reach out to those on the fringes, those who don't fit into the institutional church. "For I was hungry and you gave me something to eat, I was thirsty and you gave me something to drink, I was a stranger and you invited me in, I needed clothes and you clothed me, I was sick and you looked after me, I was in prison and you came to visit me" (Matt. 25:35-36).

Jesus had a passionate mission: "to seek and save what was lost" (Luke 19:10)—not those who were already safe on the inside but those who had no idea how to get in. His mission was to reach the lost sheep of Israel, Jewish people who did not relate to or feel welcomed into traditional temple worship. Even more specifically, he focused on those on the margins of the economic culture: the poor, the prisoners, the blind, and the oppressed (Luke 4:18). At Ginghamsburg, we've translated Jesus' mission to focus on people who are tuned out or turned off by traditional church.

Donation Versus Sacrifice

The majority of people in our churches are soft-secular people who have stopped short of being converted to a truly Christian worldview. They believe in Jesus and profess Jesus as Lord, but they still draw their meaning and security from the materialistic values of secular culture. Many people who say they believe the Bible literally, even fundamentalists, are not converted to its worldview. It's easy to profess faith and make a donation, but quite another thing to take up the cross and make a living sacrifice.

What about you? Do you measure success by the size of your organization? Have you sacrificed the revolution implicit in the kingdom of God in the name of cultural relevance?

Size is not the measure of strength. It's not how fat you are but how fit you are. Jesus must have understood this because he led a powerful movement of 120 people at the end of his earthly ministry. I'd much rather share ministry with 120 revolutionaries than lead thousands coming merely to hear how to live a bit better in their lives. Attendance is not the measure of faithfulness. Offering our bodies as living sacrifices is the measure of faithfulness (Rom. 12:1-2). Worship must challenge a person's worldview with the worldview of Christ Jesus. All the bells and whistles in our postmodern worship experiences cannot give us life if the gospel is lost. Fitness, not fatness, will determine the depth of our spiritual lives and our organization's effectiveness.

Many people in the church believe in God but draw their comfort, meaning, and security from secular culture.

The distractions on the hillside tempt us to stop short of Jesus' call to journey the way of the cross. "Whoever wants to be my disciple must deny themselves and take up their cross daily and follow me" (Luke 9:23). It is hard work to persevere through pain and the rigorous daily discipline of self-denial. The temptation is to stop short of the city of God and to set up camp at the seductive altar of the "have-it-your-way" idols. Many people in the church believe in God but draw their comfort, meaning, and security from secular culture.

Beginning my day in reflection on God's word continually challenges me to align my worldview with the worldview of Jesus. It moves me from the cult of the self to the call of the servant. I can always tell the depth of my devotion by the content of my prayers. When my prayers are, "help me accomplish . . ." or "help me achieve . . ." then my devotion is weak and shallow. As I come more to the place of, "Not my will, but yours be done," and "Lord, have mercy on me, a sinner," I am discovering again the deep places of my truest hunger and thirst.

A More Passionate Life Purpose

The practice of daily devotion renews my sense of purpose. The stronger and more compelling the *why*, the greater the creativity and energy in my life. A big *why* makes for uncompromisable integrity. This is why Jesus withdrew, to create a margin of devotion as the first act of his day. "Very early in the morning, while it was still dark, Jesus got up, left the house and went off to a solitary place, where he prayed" (Mark 1:35). Devotion was the first discipline of his day. This daily practice renewed the *why* in Jesus' life and gave him the resolution to keep his focus on his ultimate God-given date with destiny on the cross in Jerusalem. He did not waver in the face of temptation or abandon the mission amid the frustration of fickle followers.

When I get up in the morning, I shave, shower, and dress before I leave the house. In the same way, we must take the time to cleanse our spirits and dress our life visions before we begin the day's activities. I must take the time to renew God's *why* in my life so that I face the day seeking meaning over money, preferring a lasting contribution to the kingdom of God over personal accomplishment and achievement. I will not just settle for a job, because God has given me a life calling. I will set out to build a life and not just a résumé. The bigger the *why*, the greater my purpose will be.

Devotion brings me back to my true center. My work is not the center of my journey, nor is ministry the center of my life; God is. My identity is that of a servant. Jesus the Messiah didn't assume the head place at the table but assumed the servant position of washing feet. This is why we call everyone active at Ginghamsburg either "paid servants" or "unpaid servants." A "staff member" works for the money, and a "volunteer" can drop the task when it is not convenient, but servants sacrifice of themselves for the good of others. If you seek to lead or to affect others by your example, your privileges and rights decrease as your responsibility and influence increase.

Twelve years ago we began doing a Saturday evening worship celebration in order to reach more people. Now with three Saturday celebrations we are able to reach more than a thousand people who may have never felt comfortable in a Sunday morning celebration. Saturday is not a working day for the typical fifty-something with a graduate education, but that's OK, because it's not about me. I am not the master of my day but the servant of God's purpose.

Influence is not about personal accomplishment and recognition. It is about serving God by building people. It is not about us. We are servants of God Almighty, doing only what God asks of us! When you assume the kneeling posture of servant you must look up to God. You are reminded that God is not a cosmic waiter at your beck and call, waiting to be motioned over to bless your latest business deal. God revealed himself to us through Jesus as servant, and we are most like God when we are serving.

The discipline of daily devotion reminds me of my mortality. I realize that my time is short: I'm going to die! It creates a sense of urgency.

> Now listen, you who say, "Today or tomorrow we will go to this or that city, spend a year there, carry on business and make money." Why, you do not even know what will happen tomorrow. *What is your life? You are a mist that appears for a little while and then vanishes.* Instead, you ought to say, "If it is the Lord's will, we will live and do this or that." (James 4:13-15, emphasis added)

In the era after September 11, 2001, and Hurricane Katrina in 2005, we have a new awareness that our wealth cannot protect us. Such disasters remind us that no matter how technologically advanced or wealthy we become, we are not in control.

When Hurricane Katrina brought destruction to New Orleans and the Gulf Coast in August 2005, many of us became aware of what was really important. People from all over the country donated money and supplies, and even opened their homes to refugees from the afflicted area. Many traveled to New Orleans and southern Mississippi to look for survivors among the debris and help rebuild homes that had been destroyed. The devastation reminded me of Jesus' prediction of the last days:

As it was in the days of Noah, so it will be at the coming of the Son of Man. For in the days before the flood, people were eating and drinking, marrying and giving in marriage, up to the day Noah entered the ark; and they knew nothing about what would happen until the flood came and took them all away. That is how it will be at the coming of the Son of Man. (Matt. 24:37-39)

The practice of devotion renews the why in my life. "You do not even know what will happen tomorrow. What is your life? You are a mist that appears for a little while and then vanishes" (James 4:14). We're not guaranteed tomorrow, and we must do the work of Christ who calls us while it is still today. "Night is coming, when no one can work" (John 9:4).

A More Passionate Life Practice

A daily life practice of being fully present to God's presence is the foundation of all other disciplines. God speaks to those who are listening and wants to ensure the success of God's purpose through those same people. The magi who came to Bethlehem to honor the birth of Jesus took the time to discern the voice of God and then went back by another road. Jesus' earthly father, Joseph, was able to elude danger and move his family to Egypt because he was listening to God's directive. The Bible records example after example of people who received vital directives from God that would help sustain personal health, integrity, and strategic focus for the duration of the journey.

God can speak to you today in a way that guides your daily practice. It begins with getting spiritually dressed for the day. Let me show you a specific way that I have discovered best connects me to God's presence and purpose each day. See pages 44-45.

Time in the Transformation Journal: How to Use the S.O.N. Study Method

Before I open the Bible or my *Transformation Journal*, [6] I pray. I ask God to open my heart and mind to new truths, to let me see today's Scripture through God's eyes, and to help me understand it with the heart and spirit of Jesus.

Then I begin with the **S**cripture. I read it carefully and find myself tuning in particularly to the principles described and demonstrated in the text that will be most helpful to me in ministry.

Next, I make **O**bservations about the Scripture, often rereading portions of it and writing down notes about what is happening in the text or story. I also make a note of questions or ideas I have and insights into what God is doing or saying.

Last, I **N**ame the practical implications, taking a closer look at the observations and applying them to my own life and context. I look for big principles God wants me to understand as well as simple spiritual truths that challenge me to grow. God often shows me specific steps to take that day in order to align my attitude and actions with God's vision for my life.

Many times I will sum up what I've learned in a prayer of repentance, or ask for wisdom and strength for the day ahead. I take time to pray specifically for people that God has put on my heart. God uses this time to give focus to my own personal life and to the strategic direction of the ministry I lead.

Devotion in Motion

God can't steer a parked car. God is looking for people who will take their lives out of park and shift them into drive. John Wesley, the great evangelist who began the Methodist movement, talked about practical holiness and "going on to perfection." You play a part in going on to (w)holiness and creating momentum in your life. So grab that gearshift, take your life out of park, throw it into drive, and begin moving toward God's place of promise.

F 1 SAMUEL

FRIDAY: THERE MAY BE GIANTS 3/4/05

God's promise of provision does not eliminate obstacles in our walk with
him. However, God does provide deliverance as we face those challenges
with determination and confidence in God, as David did. The "giants" in
our lives will be overcome as we trust in God's power and provision.

SCRIPTURE
1 Samuel 17:1-58

OBSERVATIONS

- expect to go against Champions!
- Goliath made a crazy wager (all or nothing). No one is invinceable. Pride goes before the fall!!!
- Both sides were stuck in peacock procrastination & David got things rolling
- David ran to the battle lines/ Man of action
- vs 32 - Leadership is out in front, always acting and not reacting.
- vs 34 - David applies skills he learned as shepherd to skills he needs as warrior/leader.
- vs 37 - great faith!!!
- vs 39 - David doesn't try to fit into someone elses armour (style)

transformation journal

A ONE YEAR JOURNEY THROUGH THE BIBLE

NAME PERSONAL APPLICATIONS _____

" *I come against you in the name of the Lord almighty . . . This day the Lord will deliver you into my hands . . .* "

~ utter humility - forward action - total faith !!!

- my strength is not in my own ability or resources " it is not by sword or spear that the Lord saves; for the battle is the Lord's . . ."

- vs 50 " without a sword in his hand (David) struck down the Philistine and killed him "

- David's always "running" to the task of _____ mission,

Prayer - Father, empower me to be today who you need me to me and to be who my family believes me to be

JOURNAL QUESTIONS

•What characteristics does David demonstrate in this trial? What benefits did David's faith bring to his community?

•What "giants" are you facing right now? What actions can you take that will model David's character as you address these obstacles?

Rest Area Reflections

Read aloud the main Scriptures, Psalms 121 and 123.

1. What do those closest to you say is your passion?

2. When you "lift up your eyes to the hills," what "god" offers you immediate relief in times of stress?

3. "God is looking for people who will take their lives out of park and shift them into drive." How does this statement apply to you?

4. What is one thing God is saying to you about your own devotion?

readiness for lifelong learning

READINESS> *Preparation or availability for service, action, or progress. Prompt willingness. For example: "Readiness to resume study or continue discussions."*

In vain you rise early
and stay up late,
toiling for food to eat—
for he grants sleep to those he loves. (Ps. 127:2)

We spend more time working than on any other single activity in our brief lifetimes. Most of us will spend more time at work this week than we will with our spouses, families, or friends. And while we may get six to seven hours of sleep tonight, we will have worked eight to ten hours.

God desires for us to make the most of that time and intends for our work to have a purpose. It is not God's will that we toil in vain, anxious labor. Work is meant to be both fruitful and fulfilling. But if we are not intentional about continual growth and improvement, we can spend our entire forty-plus-year careers like the men and women of Israel who walked aimlessly in the wilderness, never to reach their destiny or taste the produce of promise.

Growth and fruitfulness go hand in hand. If I am not practicing a daily, disciplined ascent in my life's work, then I will just keep on preaching the same old sermons, singing the same old songs, and writing the same old books—and my work will not be relevant, fulfilling, or fruitful.

Remember, our destination is the house of God. In ancient Israel, the temple of God was the only place a Jewish person could go to make an honorable, excellent offering. Our journey there involves ascent, which requires that we have certain daily disciplines, or life practices, in place. Ascent never reaches a comfortable plane or plateau.

To maintain healthy forward momentum for life, I begin my day with a focused hour of **D**evotion. Jesus reminds us that the most important commandment calls us to love God with all our *heart* (Matt. 22:37). "Heart" is about who I am at the core of my being. It is the part of me that affects all my thoughts, actions, and decisions. Who I am becoming in Jesus is the most important gift that I have and can offer back to God. It is my acceptable sacrifice.

We must not forget, however, that this commandment also calls us to love God with all our *mind* (Matt. 22:37). Right after I spend about an hour listening to God (it takes me a long time, because I have a bend in my character), I spend at least a half hour in the discipline or exercise of stretching my mind. This is the practice of lifelong learning. It means I'll never get out of school. I study everything from magazine articles and books to websites and newspapers. I read and study about leadership, business, technology, history, and religion. I am interested in church trends, cultural trends, and market trends. More important, I want to know how great leaders of the past stayed both faithful and fruitful.

Jesus told us that we must sustain the never-out-of-school attitude of a child if we are truly to enter into the fruitfulness of kingdom living (Mark 10:15). Children are constantly learning, so much so that their adult caretakers can get irritated with their incessant "Why?" "Why?" and more "Why?"

For children, everything is an adventure. They can turn a bath into a Jacques Cousteau deep-sea excursion. They can find something new and interesting on every trip to the bus stop, even though they've covered the same path a hundred times. Simple objects like kitchen utensils or cardboard boxes become cherished equipment for the task at hand.

> **We must sustain the never-out-of-school attitude of a child if we are to truly enter into the fruitfulness of kingdom living.**

What we call garbage, children call gold. My regular practice is to throw empty boxes out into my garage and then flatten them every Wednesday night to put into the recycling bin outside. When our children were younger, it wasn't unusual to come home from work and find those same boxes back inside the house, magically enjoying new lives as cars, forts, and spaceships. This is an incredible habit of childhood. Adults watch television while children create.

Sometimes adults call this creativity "mischief." When I was a kid, my friends and I built a fort. We started out sawing down trees to make a log cabin, but soon discovered how much work that would entail, so we went around the neighborhood scavenging materials. We took anything we could find to complete the project. Our fort even had a brick fireplace where we built fires!

We also had an arsenal of weapons. The fort sported an artillery sling-shot I carved designs into, with a rubber inner tube for firing our projectiles. It took one kid to hold the thing and another to pull it back. I remember one night I went home and my dad said, "Mrs. Carol called me and said that Bobby came home with a cut. His forehead was bleeding. Do you know anything about that?" I replied, "Yes, Dad, but I hit him on the move. It's not easy to hit a moving target—I should get points!"

We were creative, even in our mischief! We continued our architectural pursuits for about two weeks until our parents made us tear down the fort, claiming it was a rattrap. So we moved on to another new adventure, another quest, another chance to explore, pioneer, innovate, and irritate. We kept asking, "Why?" and, "Why not?"

An Honorable, Excellent Offering

We no longer make the journey of ascent to the temple of God to offer bulls, sheep, or doves. Instead, our *life work* becomes the honorable, excellent offering we make to God. The stretching of our minds allows our work to continue on the upward ascent of God's purpose.

As I commit myself to this discipline, this practice of readiness for lifelong learning, my work will be creative, redemptive, and innovative.

> **Our whole life work, regardless of what we do, is to become an honorable, excellent offering to God.**

Creative Work

You were created to be creative. This is the work that Jesus wants to release in your life. This is what it means to be created in the image of God.

According to the opening pages of the Bible, God worked for six days and rested for one. God didn't party for six days and then work for one. Work is good or God would not have done it! Work is why we are here on planet Earth. After creating Adam, "The LORD God took the man and put him in the Garden of Eden to work it and take care of it" (Gen. 2:15). The implications here are powerful: you and I are coworkers, cocreators with God.

All work and all creativity begin in your mind. The physical manifestation of any reality begins as a thought. On a family picnic in 1959, a Dayton toolmaker named Ermal Fraze found he had no can opener. At that time, you had to use a tool called a church key to open a can of soda or beer. It was one of life's major annoyances—forgetting it could ruin many a family outing. I still have my dad's church key, which was a pain to use. If you carried it in your pocket, it could rip your pants. It could also cut your hand.

Fraze knew there had to be a better way to open a can, and being a toolmaker, he suspected the solution had something to do with rivets. He put a rivet on top of the can to create a pull-tab. Within a few years he invented, patented, and began manufacturing the "easy open" pull-tab lid that is now standard equipment. Today Fraze Pavilion, a popular outdoor entertainment venue in Kettering, Ohio, is named after this inventor whose big contribution began in his head.

You must conceive it before you can achieve it. It is why the Bible talks to us about renewing our minds (Rom. 12:1-2). To renew my mind means I must stretch it.

To renew my mind means I must stretch it.

In the beginning was the Word, and the Word was with God, and the Word was God. He was with God in the beginning. Through him all things were made. (John 1:1-3)

The first chapter of the Gospel of John tells us that the Logos, or divine intellect of God, became flesh. We know the Logos as Jesus. "The Word became flesh and made his dwelling among us" (John 1:14). The mind of God conceived an idea, and the thoughts became reality.

Like God, we must conceive before we can achieve. When Beethoven wrote the Ninth Symphony, he was totally deaf. Most people think music comes from what our ears hear, but in reality we must think it first. The symphony was first formed in Beethoven's mind. He "heard" it there, and the idea was transformed into physical reality. All physical creation begins as a thought.

Pursuit of Wisdom

The Bible repeatedly challenges us to pursue wisdom. Wisdom requires bigger thinking. It requires new thinking. Wisdom requires the exercise of a person's mind. God cannot use narrow-minded people, closed-minded people, or empty-minded people. Jesus said that you can't put new wine into old wineskins (Matt. 9:17), which have lost their ability to stretch.

I hate the discipline of stretching before my physical workouts. I'm tempted to cheat and not do it, but if I don't stretch, I will lose flexibility. God is a God of new things, calling us to sing a new song. God is looking for people with flexible minds that can receive new ideas and for people who will let those ideas be manifested into physical reality. God will not trust the valued, aged wine of redemptive wisdom to minds that are not subject to the practice of stretching, to the daily discipline of renewed thinking.

> **God will not trust the valued, aged wine of redemptive wisdom to minds that are not subject to the daily discipline of renewed thinking.**

God is no respecter of persons. God is not looking around and saying, "OK, I like Mike better, so I am going to choose Mike for my next new idea." If you are not stretching your mind, however, God is not going to waste new wine by putting it into an old skin. The obstacle to forward momentum is old thinking. Making strategic plans from old paradigms is a recipe for bursting wineskins. Remember those deadly words: "We never did it that way before." When I am stretching my mind, I am always looking forward to the next new thing.

My grandfather, with his eighty-something-year-old paradigms, was challenged by the myriad of changes going on in the world. He marveled on one occasion that I could speak on a Sunday morning at Ginghamsburg Church (outside Dayton, Ohio) and at 8:00 PM that same night in Pasadena, California, to an entirely different group of people. It was beyond his comprehension. Years later, up to the time he died, he'd ask, "Did you really do that?"

My grandfather was working from an old mental paradigm, a horse-and-buggy way of thinking. That's how he grew up. He saw his first automobile at age sixteen and bought one at age twenty-two, an incredible paradigm shift for him. He told me about his horse named Prince pulling the buggy for him and his date. He'd drop his date off at her home, fall asleep at the reins, and wake up at his farm gate because Prince knew the way back. (Try that with a car!) Little did my grandfather realize that as he was going about his daily affairs in a horse cart, Orville and Wilbur Wright—sons of a bishop in Dayton, Ohio—were stretching their paradigms and developing a new mode of travel that would make possible my same-day, cross-continental schedule.

My grandfather had never been on an airplane when he died in 1996. Neither his horse nor a car could get me to California in one afternoon. That kind of travel required a shift of thinking.

The same mind stretching was required with the invention of the cell phone. It has dramatically changed our lives at home, at school, at work, and on vacation—in approximately ten years! Until the cell phone, my telephone number was tied to a physical address. You would look up my name in a telephone book and you would read my address and then my telephone number. Yet when I was speaking in the mountains in the Czech Republic, three hours from Prague, I could take my cell phone out of my pocket and call my son in Kansas City to ask how his baseball game went. That's a paradigm shift.

Many of God's children let their minds atrophy. God, meanwhile, is looking for people who are willing to exercise their minds, to be transformed and renewed. I have the living presence of Christ dwelling within me. Jesus said that we will be able to do the things that he did and to do even greater things (John 14:12). All things are possible with God, but God will not trust his redemptive work to inflexible spirits or minds.

> **God is looking for people who are willing to exercise their minds to be transformed and renewed.**

The discipline of daily reading is work. Stretching hurts. Many people tell me, "I don't like to read." Hebrews 12:11 says, "No discipline seems pleasant at the time, but painful. Later on, however, it produces a harvest of righteousness and peace for those who have been trained by it." In other words, discipline requires sweat equity, but the benefits of discipline include a bountiful harvest. You could say the benefits are out of this world!

A God of Excellence

The sister of creativity is excellence. God worked six days, and at the end of every day said, "That was good!" At the end of the sixth day, however, God said, "That was *very* good!" God did not stop working when it was good, but only when it was *very* good (Gen. 1:31). God is a God of excellence.

A commitment to excellence honors God and builds strong self-esteem. One of the greatest needs I see in the life of the church is self-esteem, and when we are able to offer God our best, the result is healthy esteem. Psalm 127:2 says, "He grants sleep to those he loves." This implies that fruitful, excellent labor results in restful sleep. When our work reflects the excellence of God, we get to the end of the day and just want to high-five God, saying, "We did good today, God!" We can go to sleep at night knowing that we are getting an incredible return on our investment. This partnership affords us a strong sense of contribution, personal worth, and satisfaction.

Excellence is not about comparing ourselves or our work with the work of others. We should not look around and say, "I am doing better than that person." We have a higher standard. The company doesn't set our goal. The union doesn't determine the pace of our work. We work by God's standards.

When I speak at conferences, people ask me which one of my books is my best one. I always reply, "I haven't written my best book yet." I haven't preached my best sermon yet; I haven't sung my best song yet; and I haven't made my best offering to God yet. I am on a journey of ascent. I am always looking up. My sense of focus comes from my daily discipline of lifelong learning. From a biblical perspective, the best is yet to come.

God always saves the best for last. Remember Jesus' first water-to-wine miracle? Most party hosts served the best wine first and then brought the inferior product out when everyone was a little tipsy and couldn't tell the difference. Not so with Jesus. "You have saved the best until now" (John 2:10). This is what the journey of ascent is about. It just keeps getting better. Even the prospect of death is no threat, for the best is yet to come.

I don't want to get old, but I do want to become aged like good wine. There is a difference. We all have God-dreams for our educations, careers, and marriages, yet many people I know give up on those dreams by the time they're thirty. They begin to grow prematurely old in mind and spirit, losing the ability to stay fresh and flexible in the ascent. By age fifty they want to retire to the beach and stop contributing to God's dream for the world. That kind of retirement is not a biblical option. It is the consequence of people losing their God-inspired momentum.

Moses, a lifelong learner himself, wasn't even ripe for God's picking until he was eighty years old. At the full-bodied age of eighty, he had grown sufficiently in spirit and in wisdom to maximize the fruitfulness of his leadership.

Many people quit before they realize their most productive years of service. God's best is yet to come! Consider these lifelong learners:

- Michelangelo, at the age of fifty-nine, learned a new method of painting upside down, and painted *The Creation of Adam* on the ceiling of the Sistine Chapel.
- At age sixty-six Colonel Harland Sanders started the Kentucky Fried Chicken chain.
- At age sixty-nine Ronald Reagan was elected to his first term as president, the oldest person to be elected president until he topped his own record and was reelected at seventy-three.
- Golda Meir became prime minister of Israel at age seventy-one.
- Nelson Mandela became the first black president of South Africa at the age of seventy-five, after being a political prisoner for twenty-seven years.
- John Glenn, at the age of seventy-seven, made his second trip into outer space.
- At age eighty-one, Benjamin Franklin was elected a delegate to the U.S. Constitutional Convention, leading our country on a very different course than it might have taken otherwise.
- Grandma Moses took up painting in her seventies, and created her most famous painting, *The Old Checkered House*, at age eighty-two.
- Well into his eighties, Paul Harvey continues to get up every morning to record his daily radio broadcast heard around the globe.
- At the age of one hundred, Strom Thurmond completed his eighth term as a U.S. senator.

Just as these achievers were all lifelong learners, you and I must never leave school. We must each practice the daily discipline of lifelong learning. We must hold on to the inquisitive nature of the child within so that we don't miss the incredible wonders of the kingdom of God. Mediocrity does not honor God.

Mediocrity does not honor God.

I love Jesus' demonstration of excellence when he healed the blind man of Bethesda (Mark 8:22-25). Jesus spat, rubbed his spit into the man's eyes, and then asked, in essence, "Well, how is it?" The blind man replied, "I can see colors and movement, but everything is kind of blurry. People look like they are trees walking around, but it's OK—really!"

Jesus said, "Hold on. We are not into 'OK' here. Let's give it another go-around." Jesus touched him once more, and the job was complete—20/20 vision. Jesus didn't quit until the job was done, and done with excellence. Jesus wasn't into mediocrity, and to bear the name of Jesus requires that we pursue the excellence of God as well. It doesn't get any better than when your time to die comes and you are able to say to the Father, "I have finished with excellence the work you sent me to do."

Redemptive Work

How many hours will you spend doing your job this week? The majority of us will put in a minimum of forty hours, with many of us working fifty and beyond.

What is the purpose of work from God's perspective? Work is an act of worship. "Therefore, I urge you, brothers and sisters, in view of God's mercy, to offer your bodies as a living sacrifice, holy and pleasing to God—this is true worship" (Rom. 12:1). The Greek word for *worship* is the same word used for *service*. Some Bibles translate *worship* here as *work*. To worship is to render physical service. Your work is your spiritual service to God. To work is to worship and to worship is to work; it's bringing an honorable, excellent offering to God.

Our culture has reduced the idea of worship to a one-hour weekly event, when it is really a daily endeavor involving all of our work. The word *liturgy* comes from two Greek words: *laos* (people) and *ergon* (work). Liturgy means people at work. The purpose of our work is to render service to God. It is to be a daily part of God's redemptive work in the world.

The Psalms of Ascent remind us of the potential distractions and idolatries that can take us off the path and keep us from reaching the ultimate purpose of God for our lives. Psalm 127 calls our attention to one of them: "vain labor" or fruitless work, which is any work you do that is not part of God's redemptive plan in the world.

What makes the difference? It is futile work if you, rather than God, are at the center. It is "in vain" when the motive of work is money. Jesus called this the bigger-barns syndrome. He told the story of a man whose entire motive for working was to make money. After he made a lot of money, he still couldn't see beyond himself as the center of the universe. "He said, 'This is what I'll do. I will tear down my barns and build bigger ones, and there I will store my surplus grain. And I'll say to myself, "You have plenty of grain laid up for many years. Take life easy; eat, drink and be merry" ' " (Luke 12:18-19).

Jesus called that man a fool, and later said, "Do not work for food that spoils, but for food that endures to eternal life, which the Son of Man will give you" (John 6:27).

Not long ago I spoke with a businessman in his forties, living in our community and working in the field of engineering. "You know what I've always wanted to do with my life?" he remarked to me. "I've always wanted to teach at a community college. That is my ultimate goal. When I retire, I'm going to teach at a community college."

I replied, "You mean, if you could do anything in the world right now, you would teach at a community college?"

"Yes," he said.

"Then why are waiting until you retire?" I asked. "You could die in a year—who knows when you're going to die? Why don't you just go do it now? You have a master's degree; just go teach in a community college."

You know what he said to me? "I can't afford to."

When our work is driven by the monetary return on our labors, then we are really saying, "My security comes from money, not God's promise of provision." When we do this, we become fearful of the very calling God has placed in our hearts and we squander the passion God has placed within us. Saying, "I believe in God, but I trust money for my security," is today's version of the bigger-barns syndrome.

When I went into ministry, my first salary was $3,800 a year. Both my parents and Carolyn's parents said, "You're crazy." Carolyn's dad, who was a Christian, said, "Well, you have a great heart, Mike, but how are you going to feed my grandbabies?"

Amazingly, I poured myself into the passion God placed in my heart, and the blessings God provided for me have potentially surpassed what I would have made in the business world.

Many people master the art of making a living but never discover the joy of living.

Why do so many of us profess our belief in God but trust money for our security? Faith is the ultimate expression of the object of your trust. We've only been given this one life. To waste that life because money is the source of your well-being and provision is vain worship. Many people master the art of making a living but never discover the joy of living.

Life is too short to work at a job only for the purpose of earning a living. I want a calling, not a job. I want to build a life—not a résumé! God has placed a great passion in your heart. Pursue that passion with everything that you profess, and trust God's provision.

As I write this chapter, I am reading the book *The Smartest Guys in the Room* by Bethany McLean and Peter Elkind. It profiles Kenneth Lay, who was the founder and CEO of Enron, the fifth-biggest company in the world. Enron went belly-up and took all the employees' retirement money. The authors describe Lay as a person of *intended* integrity.

> Lay seemed to care deeply about bettering the world. He spent much of his time on philanthropy; in Houston, he was the go-to man for charitable works, raising and giving away millions. He spoke often about corporate values. And he was openly religious. "Everybody knows that I personally have a very strict code of personal conduct that I live by," he once told an interviewer for a religious magazine called *The Door*. "This code is based on Christian values." [1]

How could a man who apparently held such high standards destroy the trust of thousands of employees and investors and send a quake through the world's economy? Jesus said that none of us is able to serve two masters (Matt. 6:24). You cannot work for both God and money. Somewhere along the way the idol of vain labor distracted Mr. Lay. "More money" became the driving mantra of his journey of ascent. When Lay discovered that the two people who led one of Enron's divisions were engaging in criminal acts, he refused to fire them. According to McLean and Elkind, Kenneth Lay stated openly at a company board meeting that these directors earned the company too much money to let them go. [2]

Kenneth Lay seemed to be working "for food that spoils." The measure of work is not the wealth it produces for us, but the opportunities it provides for service. Our work becomes an honorable, excellent offering to God as we contribute to the well-being of others. This is true worship!

The Priority of People

We work for the benefit of others. One of the Psalms of Ascent reminds us of the motivation for this life journey. "For the sake of my friends and of all the people, / I will say, 'Peace be within you.' / For the sake of the house of the LORD our God, / I will seek your prosperity" (Ps. 122:8-9).

The gospel is counter to many of the cultural values portrayed in reality programs such as *The Apprentice* and *Survivor*, where the goal is to gain advantage and ultimate victory over your teammates. Work must never exploit people for the purpose of personal profit or selfish gain.

When I am actively participating in the redemptive work of Jesus, my labors will add value, enhance quality of life, and promote connectedness in relationship. When my work is not an act of worship, it will result in the construction of a tower of Babel. "Then they said to each other, 'Come, let us build ourselves a city, with a tower that reaches to the heavens, so that we may make a name for ourselves' " (Gen. 11:4). Whereas bigger barns are all about more money, towers of Babel are all about more me. My achievement, my recognition, and my personal success become the driving, motivating force behind my work, rather than my desire to make a lasting contribution to God's greater redemptive purpose.

Ross is a Jesus follower and a passionate car salesperson whose sales record is always near the top at the dealership where he works. Now here's the paradox: several years ago he refused to sell me a car that I would have used credit to buy. Ross was convinced the acquisition would overstretch my finances. He truly seeks the prosperity of others, as the psalmist describes, even at the cost of his own commission.

By their actions toward others, people like Ross demonstrate the power of God. As I emphasized in the previous chapter, whatever we do or fail to do for people, we do or fail to do for God. We want to be among the ones that Jesus welcomes with great reward: "Come, you who are blessed by my Father; take your inheritance, the kingdom prepared for you since the creation of the world" (Matt. 25:34). It's as we respond to people's true needs—whether hunger, thirst, homelessness, sickness, or even financial imprisonment—that we truly serve the God we name.

We're all going to die, and the offering we make to God is all that will live beyond us. Your worship is far more than the songs you sing in church. Worship is the honorable, excellent offering you're making to God through your work as part of God's redemptive purpose in the world.

Worship is the honorable, excellent offering you're making to God through your work as part of God's redemptive purpose in the world.

The greater the sacrifice we are willing to make, the broader the scope of influence God will allow us to have.

A Poured-Out Sacrament

When we daily offer our work to God as an act of worship, God makes it a poured-out sacrament in the lives of others. "Whoever finds their life will lose it, and whoever loses their life for my sake will find it" (Matt. 10:39). The greater the sacrifice we are willing to make, the broader the scope of influence God will allow us to have in the lives of other people.

The practice of going to work every day provides the opportunity for you to be a poured-out sacrament in the lives of other people. When I place myself in God's hands, God is able to use my offering as squeezed-out grapes and broken bread, sustenance in the lives of other people.

When I began preaching at worship celebrations on Saturday night, it really wasn't a terribly difficult choice, even though I previously had both Mondays and Saturdays off. Nobody told me I had to start working on Saturdays. The idea came when I prayed, "How much more of a blessing could I be in this short lifetime if I am willing to work on Saturdays?" My income didn't change when I started working Saturdays, but I was able to be a greater influence for God. That was a sacrifice I was willing to make. In the hands of Jesus, I become a sacrament in the lives of other people.

For me, the harder decision was not the initial one of launching a Saturday night celebration. The key is *staying* in the hand of God on a daily basis, and that's not as easy as it sounds. When I fail to stay available to God by neglecting to practice my daily disciplines, I become more like a marble than a grape, inflexible and devoid of anything to offer others. You just can't squeeze life out of a marble.

The disciplined, daily practice of lifelong learning makes me more useful in God's service to others. Gordon McDonald reminds us, "The development of the mind makes it possible for men and women to be servants to the generation in which they live."[3]

Do you know why God chose Moses? Even at eighty years old, Moses was a lifelong learner. Moses was strategic to God's purpose because he was a lifelong student of his culture and time. "Moses was educated in all the wisdom of the Egyptians and was powerful in speech and action" (Acts 7:22). We must begin our day by stretching our spirits in reflective study and active listening through God's word. Like Moses, we must then stretch our minds through the study of the ideas, mores, and preferences of the cultures in which we live and work, positioning ourselves to make the most honorable, excellent offering to God possible.

Innovative Work

It is amazing to note Jesus' methods of innovation as he went about doing the work of God. "Having said this, he spit on the ground, made some mud with the saliva, and put it on the man's eyes. 'Go,' he told him, 'wash in the Pool of Siloam.' . . . So the man went and washed, and came home seeing" (John 9:6-7). In Kim Miller's book *Designing Worship* (Group Publishing, 2004) she asks, "What does it take to make a miracle happen?"

> From our own limited perspectives, we imagine God with sparkling magic potions carefully arranged in a heavenly toolbox. Maybe with a few wands thrown in for the really tough jobs. God's best work, however, has always been done with amazingly ordinary stuff—water, mud, spit, a piece of stale bread, a barn, a teenage girl, twelve dysfunctional disciples. God uses ordinary objects in regular places with everyday people.[4]

During America's industrial age, Dayton, Ohio, was known as a center of innovation. From its poets (Paul Laurence Dunbar) to its pilots (the Wright brothers), Dayton looked to the future. Not only pull-top beverage cans (as mentioned earlier in this chapter), but cellophane tape, the cash register, the movie camera and projector, the parachute, the computing scale, and the electric automobile starter were all invented in Dayton.

An economic report released in early 2005, however, reported Ohio as being next to last in the rankings of states that are creating new jobs (Michigan was last). The economies of Ohio and Michigan are dependent on the industries that support Detroit and the automobile industry. The area once known as the "industrial belt," for its mastery of the industrial age, is now referred to as the "rust belt," because we have not yet figured how to make the transition to the age of information and technology.

Compare that to the church that has not made the transition from an age of traditional-rural-family-based values to an age of pop-urban-individual-based values. Mark Driscoll, a young pastor in Seattle, effectively makes the case for continual innovation in his book *The Radical Reformission*: "Churches have to continually examine and adjust their musical styles, websites, aesthetics, acoustics, programming, and just about everything but their Bible in an effort to effectively communicate the gospel to as many people as possible in the cultures around them." [5] Our world is constantly changing, and God is continually creating new wine. You can't put today's wine into yesterday's wineskins.

Innovation often requires "unLearning" as well as learning. My book *UnLearning Church* focuses on the importance of "unLearning" old habits and old paradigms that prevent people and organizations from being attuned to God's new plans.[6] We must "forget what lies behind and strain forward to what lies ahead" if we are to grow and ascend toward God's purpose for our life and work (see Phil. 3:13). When you quit growing, you quit being useful to God. When you quit stretching your spirit and your mind, you plateau. You leave the path of ascent, and your life and work will be neither fulfilling nor fruitful.

People who are committed to the lifelong discipline of learning continue to add value to the endeavors they are committed to. Most people can readily identify the obstacles and problems inherent in any organization.

> **Innovation often requires "unLearning" as well as learning.**

Take, for example, the twelve spies Moses sent out as advance scouts into the promised land. Ten members of the board readily identified all the "why we can't" barriers, but Joshua and Caleb were able to find the "why we can" solutions and lead the way.

I will never put anyone who is not committed to a rugged discipline of lifelong learning on our staff or church board. Everyone I work with must be committed to becoming an expert in God's future. The senior management team and leadership board of our church travel together around the country to study the best innovative practices of other ministries.

Your Own Practice of Lifelong Learning

Consider these three practices of lifelong learning: reading, observing, and doing.

Read

First, you should always be reading something. I often ask people who are successful and faithful, who are moving forward on the journey of ascent, what they are reading. I want to know what is feeding and inspiring them.

When I asked Bill Weikert, the chair of our board and a co-owner of a local company, what he was reading, he mentioned *The Smartest Guys in the Room*, about the Enron scandal. He told me I ought to read it, so I got the book. As you can tell from my comments in this chapter, I didn't just buy the book—I read it and learned from it!

I want to move with people who are moving. You must always be reading something and must always be ready to share with someone how it is helping you become better.

Observe

Second, train yourself to observe. The Bible says wisdom cries aloud from the streets (Prov. 1:20). I am observing all the time, seeking opportunities to learn. I am looking for pioneers, older people who are ahead of me making honorable, excellent offerings to God.

A lot of people start out as pioneers until life becomes a little dangerous. That is how Pittsburgh was founded. A lot of people in those posh, big, civilized eastern cities like Boston and Philadelphia proclaimed,

"We're going west!" They got as far as Pittsburgh only to discover that people who were not excited about sharing the land already occupied Ohio. The going would be dangerous from there on out, and the pioneers quickly became settlers as they realized the cost involved.

I am not attracted to settlers. I am observing older people who are faithfully continuing the ascent ahead of me. I am watching for younger people who show signs of budding innovation. I am observing the best leaders and communicators in multiple venues.

When God called me to be a preacher, I didn't study preachers. I saw too much mediocrity there. I studied effective comedians! Richard Pryor and Bill Cosby were two of my mentors in communication skills. I figured that anyone who could talk for an hour and have people pay $75 a head to hear them had to have something going on. I considered it a compliment when someone told me I reminded him of a white Richard Pryor.

Anytime I have an opportunity to watch a comedy special on television, I watch it and study everything the comedian does. It's not that I want to be funny; I simply want to learn more about engaging an audience.

The Bible tells us to take the good and separate the bad (Matt. 10:16; 13:24-30), so I am continually observing the people who are great leaders and communicators. Name your circle of observation. These people become part of your mentoring network. Who are the great leaders and strong communicators that you can learn from?

Do

We learn the most from hands-on experience. We retain the most of what we read, see, and hear when we are able to practice by doing.

Writing the first edition of this book in 2004 was a major learning curve for me, as it was the first book I wrote on a computer. I was fifty-three years old, but was just a baby in light of the potential for my thinking. All the books I wrote previously were inked out by hand on yellow legal pads. I wrote *Out on the Edge*[7] in the 1990s about media and worship. It was one of the first Christian books with an accompanying interactive CD-ROM. The *Wall Street Journal* did a whole-page story on that book and Ginghamsburg's experience as a multimedia, multisensory church.[8] Yet look at the irony: I wrote a book about ministry entering the media age, but I used longhand on a yellow legal pad!

Writing a book with word-processing software was a new experience, but we learn by doing, and I was committed to the challenging—albeit often painful—discipline of relearning how to "write."

"No discipline seems pleasant at the time, but painful. Later on, however, it produces a harvest of righteousness and peace for those who have been trained by it" (Heb. 12:11). In other words, discipline is painful for a while, but it has one heaven of a payoff!

What will you do today to develop further your own discipline of life-long learning? You've got only one life, which will last but a few years on this earth. That life was created to be an honorable, excellent offering to God, and the greatest expression of worship is your work. Commit yourself every day to the discipline of learning—and "unLearning"—to keep you moving forward on your journey of ascent.

Rest Area Reflections

Read aloud the main Scripture, Psalm 127.

1. God desires our work to be fruitful and fulfilling, but we aren't all experiencing this benefit. How would you describe your work or day job?
   - Just a paycheck

   - More frustrating than fulfilling

   - Enjoyable, but I don't see how it's fruitful for God

   - Fruitful and fulfilling

2. As a form of worship, our work should always add value to the lives of others. How do you see your work adding value?

3. Are you committed to being a lifelong learner? What could you read or study that would advance God's vision for the world?

4. What do you hear God saying to you (so far) as you build momentum for life?

investing in key relationships

RELATIONSHIP> *The state of being related; the mutual exchange between two people or groups who have dealings with one another; kinship.*

Your wife will be like a fruitful vine within your house; your children will be like olive shoots around your table. Yes, this will be the blessing for the man who fears the LORD. (Ps. 128:3-4)

I can't remember the last time I cried. Like many stoic people, I often find myself holding my emotions in check as I keep my eyes focused on the task at hand. I feel a certain responsibility as husband, father, son, and pastor to do what I have to do and process it later. This compartmentalization usually works for me, although it certainly did not during one traumatic week several years ago.

It started one night with a 12:45 AM phone call from my sister in Cincinnati. "Dad just drove himself to the hospital," Gayle said. "He had chest pains, his blood pressure was 212/110, and they might have to do emergency surgery in two hours." By 1:05 AM, I was racing down I-75 toward Cincinnati. A half hour later I arrived at the hospital, where Gayle and I kept vigil through the night.

In the end, Dad did not need emergency surgery, but seeing my eighty-year-old father lying anxious and confused in that hospital bed was extremely difficult for us. We remembered how, just a few months before, he had driven from Florida to Ohio in a day. Even more difficult were the doctor's words about the low survival rates of the various surgeries being considered for him. I began to think of things I would say at his funeral.

Still, I did not cry. "I will do whatever I have to do!" I told myself.

Later that same day, I went on our church's men's retreat. I had helped plan it and was scheduled to speak. It was Friday evening, and I was in the hotel room with our teaching pastor, Mike Bowie, and guest speaker Rudy Rasmus from Houston, Texas, when my cell phone rang.

"Where are you?" My wife's voice broke on the other end.

My first thought was that something happened to my Dad. Carolyn began to cry hysterically. Mike and Rudy could hear her deep anguish over the phone. Not knowing what was wrong, they began to pray.

"Toby's dead!" Carolyn finally blurted out. Toby was our miniature schnauzer, who was just four months shy of sixteen years old. I had given him to Carolyn for one of her significant birthdays. She had told me that he was the best present I had ever given her. In recent months Toby had suffered some blindness and various older-dog maladies, but was still a cherished companion in our empty human nest.

"He's dead, Michael!" Carolyn continued. "I let him out into the backyard for a few minutes, and he didn't come in. I went out into the snow and found him lifeless in the fishpond."

Toby represents many different transitions and memories in my family's collective history. He was around when my grandparents were still alive. He was the family pet of our children's years at home—children now grown and living in different parts of the country. He was our faithful companion whose image marks the photographs of sacred family passages and memorable Christmas pasts. He sat next to me as I wrote each one of my books in our navy blue leather chair.

Quickly explaining to Mike and Rudy what had happened, I grabbed my luggage, threw it in my car, and headed for home. There was no time to truly feel my emotions—only the urgency to be who I needed to be for Carolyn and for the care of the dog. I knew the drill: "I will do what I have to do . . . for my wife, for Toby, for the family." During the thirty-five-minute drive home from the retreat site, my mind was racing. "It's February in Ohio. I need to do something with the dog tonight. How can I dig a burial hole in the near-frozen ground?" I tried to push away visions of Toby paddling helplessly in the water and then drowning—things a good dad should never allow to happen.

My thoughts weren't clear and orderly; they were more like flashes that swirled around my mind. Through the blur, I was aware of my deep sense of responsibility: "I will be who I have to be. I will do what I have to do. I am strong. I am a husband . . . dad . . . man . . . pastor . . . leader."

My dad's hospitalization, less than twenty-four hours previously, had left me feeling numb. I was still numb as I drove home.

I'll always remember the picture of what happened next. I walked through the door and saw Carolyn sitting on the couch in the family room. She held Toby, cradled in his blanket, on her lap.

That's when I lost it. I held our dead dog and nuzzled his ear, and I began to cry. It was a long, deep, painful mourning. A tidal wave of emotion engulfed me. I felt an all-encompassing, gut-wrenching pain—the kind of pain I imagine people in my church experience over a child's death, cancer, abusive relationships, or addictions—feelings I typically insulate myself from. I agonized not just over Toby's death, but over the senseless deaths that result from murderous terrorist attacks, and over the quarter-million people who were washed away in the December 2004 tsunami just a few weeks earlier. Grief-stricken, I got in touch with my own human condition of helplessness as I cried, "Why, God? Why?"

Meaning and Relationships

The crisis of sickness and death is the ultimate reminder of life's true meaning, and we remember what really matters. We are created for relationships. We learn life and faith through the experience of family and friends.

> **We learn life and faith through the experience of family and friends.**

Relationship Rituals

We experience life through a pattern of relationship rituals that is different for each of us. Have you ever paused to consider the rituals that frame the relationships in your own extended family? I remember riding in the car every Sunday to my grandparents' house for lunch. My uncle's family was usually there too. I can still picture the seating arrangement in that crowded back-porch-turned-year-round-dining-room of my grandparents' home. My grandfather was always at one end of the red-checked plastic tablecloth and my dad at the other. I sat next to Granddaddy and across from Uncle Thomas. Beginning in 1996, when my grandfather died, holiday meals found me in his former seat, with my father still at his post on the other end of the table.

Listening to the tribal stories around that table, I learned my identity. Through our relationship rituals, we transmitted values from one generation to another. It was there I heard stories of our family's faith, and there my grandmother taught me my first Bible verse, John 3:16. As a very young child I was sitting at that table when I first met a person of another race—a Japanese seminary student. Our family played board games and—with equal intensity— debated political ideology around that table.

The family table is where I discovered the sacrament of life.

I experienced good and bad, function and dysfunction. Most of all, I learned that God loved the world of people—all the people that I had experienced and talked about at that table. Through the relationships around that table, God's love took human form. The family table is where I discovered the sacrament of life.

Although holiday meals can make me sleepy, with each passing year I'm less tempted to nap when my family is making precious holiday memories. I force myself to stay awake and look around, remembering that nothing will last forever. I want to breathe in the awe and wonder of witnessing my children interacting with their grandparents. I don't want to miss the experience of these relationships while I'm living in the middle of them.

We miss out on life and meaning if we are not making relationships a priority on any given day. People are created for relationships, and it's in the context of our relationship rituals that we find meaning.

We miss out on life and meaning if we are not making relationships a priority on any given day.

The Value of Life

I can't control life. I can't even control what happens in my own backyard! I want to think that I can always make my family safe, but look what happened to my beloved pet. I am still dealing with feelings of guilt over my own responsibility: Why did I install that fishpond? Why didn't I put a fence around it?

I'm facing the age-old quandary of Job: Why do bad things happen to good people? The day after my meltdown, I read about Moses' death and the grief of the Hebrew community, and I wrote in my journal, "Maybe death is what makes life so valuable!"

Life repeatedly informs us that we are not in control. Devastating events like Hurricane Katrina in 2005 or the shooting at Virginia Tech in 2007 remind us that no matter how wealthy or advanced our society is, we cannot control the aging of a human life, the actions of other people, or the groaning of the earth. Our wealth and technology ultimately cannot protect or save us.

People Matter

Life is not about stuff we own or accumulate. It is not even about personal accomplishment. Life is about people. We can replace stuff, but we can't replace people!

Carolyn repeatedly asked herself the question, "Would I have done anything different in the weeks before Toby died?" Her answer was, "I would have held him more."

Carolyn takes her life's work very seriously, and thus she was working on the computer in an upstairs bedroom of our home that fateful night. She sent a last e-mail at 9:27 PM and went downstairs to let Toby out. Her plan was to hold him in his blanket and warm him up when he came inside—but he never came back.

> **Life is not about our accumulated stuff or personal accomplishment. Life is about people.**

Her thought about spending more time to hold Toby led Carolyn to other thoughts as she reflected later in the week. "Here's the question it makes me ask," she said. "Am I spending enough time with my mother?" Carolyn had not seen her eighty-five-year-old mother in two months. Toby's death had served as a sobering reminder of life's true meaning.

Margins

In Psalm 128 (another Psalm of Ascent), notice the integration of work and relationships as an expression of worship. Like D-R-I-V-E, the psalm begins with Devotion to God. "Blessed are all who fear the LORD, / who walk in obedience to him" (v. 1). Every day, "Devotion" is my act of getting in touch with God. What happens as a result? "You will eat the fruit of your labor; / blessings and prosperity will be yours" (v. 2). When you fear the Lord, your work will become an honorable, excellent offering to God.

The psalm then moves from work to relationships. The two don't compete against, but complement each other. "Your wife will be like a fruitful vine within your house; / your children will be like olive shoots around your table. / Yes, this will be the blessing for the man who fears the LORD" (vv. 3-4).

When the object of our devotion is right, our work and relationships unite as an honorable, excellent offering to God. Think of the amount of time and energy we spend at work and with our loved ones each week, compared to the paltry hour we spend at church. God is not nearly as interested in the little religious ceremonies we call worship services as in how we live our lives day to day. Our work and our relationships are not separate from our relationship with God, but are the primary expressions of this relationship. They are the truest demonstrations of our worship.

> **Our work and our relationships are the truest demonstrations of our worship.**

Do you want to honor God—to bring an honorable, excellent offering? We do this by creating and maintaining margins for the key relationships in our lives. On a piece of paper, the margin is the empty space on the side. Margins in life are the blank spaces on our calendars—our sacred spaces. You dare not allow your margin for relationships to fill up. When we keep open spaces and time for relationships, we honor God.

Isaiah 5:8 says, "Ah, you who join house to house, / who add field to field, / until there is room for no one but you, / and you are left to live alone / in the midst of the land!" (NRSV). In other words, all you do is work. You are consumed in expanding your property (joining house to house). You burn the candle at both ends to ensure a good harvest for your fields.

We are created for relationships, and relationships are developed in the margins of our lives. Acts of kindness are done in the margins. When you don't have any margins, people leave you alone because you are always on the edge.

> **Relationships are developed in the margins of our lives.**

Trouble in the Margins

We get into trouble when we allow our work to fill the margins that are meant for our relationships. That's what

72

happened to Carolyn and me. We allowed ministry to become a priority over our relationship, so that after twenty years of marriage we looked at each other and didn't know each other, let alone like each other! The problem was that we had allowed zero daily margins for our relationship.

This is a mistake of youth. Many people fall into it, as did Carolyn and I. Unfortunately, too many of us don't figure out the problem until we are forty or fifty. Some never get it. In our youth, we discover that it is easier to focus on a task that can't scream at us and say, "You aren't meeting my needs!" Tasks reward us without talking back. Without realizing it, we learn to focus on tasks rather than relationships.

> **In our youth, we discover that it is easier to focus on a task that can't scream at us and say, "You aren't meeting my needs!"**

In marriages, it begins around the time you are supposedly making a commitment of lifelong time and energy to your partner. When you are dating, you are focused on building a relationship. You are finding out what pleases the other person. You explore what the other person likes and dislikes, and you listen to each other's deepest needs. Then, you become engaged. At that point you no longer focus on the relationship; you center on planning the wedding, a task that begins to swallow up valuable energy formerly invested in the relationship. When Carolyn and I became engaged, we were no longer listening to each other's thoughts and sharing our dreams. Rather, we were doing chores: running all over Cincinnati picking out patterns for china we would rarely eat on and silverware I've yet to see! Even choosing a cake became a complex task, not to mention the dresses and tuxedos; the gifts for groomsmen and bridesmaids; the rehearsal dinner; reservations at the chapel at Miami University, where we married; and arrangements for the reception. Whew!

Then we got married and said, "OK, as soon as we get out of school, we'll have time for each other and we'll work more on our relationship." We didn't.

By now a pattern has developed—a practice of postponement that you too may have experienced. "After grad school we're sure to get more time together," you say to each other; then, "When we get away on vacation this summer, we'll have two weeks just for us." The vacation flies by and soon you're rationalizing again: "When you get settled in your new job, then we'll work on the relationship."

It's not long before children come into the picture, and soon this habit of relational postponement is the only way you know to function. From toddler tears to the high-school years, there are no real breaks in the parenting schedule, no weeks when the kids turn to you and say, "We'll take care of ourselves this week; why don't you two work on your relationship?" Finally, when the kids leave and the nest is empty, you wake up one morning and look at each other and say, "Who the heck are you?"

Living Fully Today

In 1938, Thornton Wilder wrote a Pulitzer Prize–winning play called *Our Town*. It's a perennial favorite in high schools. It tells the story of a young woman named Emily who dies and is given permission to return to the earth for one memorable day. She can pick any day from her lifetime and relive it moment by moment.

Emily chooses to go back on her twelfth birthday because she remembered it as a happy day. She is soon frustrated, however, at the indifference of those she loves. She wishes to engage in life with them but painfully observes that they are just going through the motions, taking each moment totally for granted. As she stands by and watches her birthday take place, she tries to stop it because she can't take it anymore!

She had been reliving her special day, and yet no one was experiencing the significant moments. People weren't even looking at one another. Emily cries out, "I can't. I can't go on. It goes so fast. We don't have time to look at one another. . . . Do any human beings ever realize life while they live it?—every, every minute?"[1]

Jesus cautioned about this human tendency. "Therefore do not worry about tomorrow, for tomorrow will worry about itself. Each day has enough trouble of its own" (Matt. 6:34). And James 4:14 states, "What is your life? You are a mist that appears for a little while and then vanishes." The prophetic implication: live fully today.

Each of us is responsible for our own schedule, for how we will order today. If I don't prioritize how and with whom I spend my time, circumstances and other people will decide for me.

> **If I don't prioritize how and with whom I spend my time, circumstances and other people will decide for me.**

My intentional schedule becomes my offering to God. I must prioritize how I will spend my days, how I will create and maintain margins for relationships.

Think about your life today. What relational disciplines do you need in order to make an honorable, excellent offering to God? Relationships provide us with ultimate meaning, but we must create the margins wherein they will flourish.

Mentoring

God's strategy for the transmission of faith and biblical values to future generations involves mentoring-based relationships. It's God's plan for passing the DNA of the kingdom of God from person to person, generation to generation.

The transmission is fragile, however, and the handoff has great potential for a fumble. Judges 2:10-11 reminds us: "After that whole generation had been gathered to their ancestors, another generation grew up who knew neither the LORD nor what he had done for Israel. Then the Israelites did evil in the eyes of the LORD and served the Baals." The people faithfully served God during Joshua's lifetime, but the next generation did not maintain the values of their parents.

There is a critical difference between ideals and values. Ideals are what you want; values are what you truly live. Your ideals might be that you raise your children to be faithful followers of Jesus, go to college, have fruitful and fulfilling careers, and marry persons of faith, integrity, and intelligence. Values, however, are the real-life priorities that determine your (and their) actual choices. Values are demonstrated through our behaviors more than our cognitive beliefs. The challenge is that our values and our beliefs don't always line up: "For I have the desire to do what is good, but I cannot carry it out. For I do not do the good I want to do, but the evil I do not want to do—this I keep on doing" (Rom. 7:18-19). How you invest your time, your energy, and your money are the true indicators of your values.

> **How you invest your time, energy, and money are the true indicators of your values.**

Many people in the church have biblical ideals but live secular values. They are functional atheists. In the end, our children will inherit and live out our values, not our ideals.

75

The People in Your Heart

Our first mentoring responsibility is to the people we have in our hearts—our children or those who are emotionally close to home. Psalm 128 reminds us of the priority of the home and the values transmitted therein: "Your wife will be like a fruitful vine within your house; / your children will be like olive shoots / around your table" (Ps. 128:3).

The women and men who fear the Lord make the mentoring of their families in the values of the kingdom a major priority. This means my family becomes a higher priority than the church where I work. When I keep God's practical life disciplines on a daily basis, I will make time priorities for my spouse and children, knowing that those closest to us will be adopting our values.

When our son, Jonathan, was in college, Carolyn and I moved to Philadelphia for five weeks to experience his last baseball season at the University of Pennsylvania. From a career perspective this might not have been perceived as a wise decision. The church was in a 20 percent growth climb. It was the Lenten season, leading toward Easter, a busy, important time of year for a pastor! But what is my first "profession"? It's transmitting my kingdom of God values to the next generation.

I had never seen my son hit a college home run. He hit three that year, and I saw all three. Every day I showed up on campus to pitch to Jonathan as part of his practice regimen, much as I had pitched to him in the batting cage at home before he went to college.

Our children follow our values, and our truest values are demonstrated through our time priorities. Parenting is a lifelong intentional time schedule, a career of mentorship. We made a huge investment of our time in Jonathan that spring, and it was a blast. We made memories so precious that Carolyn and I wouldn't trade them for anything.

People need to see leaders who demonstrate the priorities of the kingdom of God in their primary relationships.

An amazing side effect of this whole scenario was that the church continued to grow without me. People need to see leaders who demonstrate the priorities of the kingdom of God in their primary relationships.

It's important to note that the opposite effect could have occurred. What a burden we would have put upon Jonathan if he had been out there trying to prove himself to us, to get our attention, or to free himself from negative self-talk we had instilled into his life.

A 2002 movie called *The Rookie* is based on the story of baseball great Jim Morris. Repeated injuries force this aspiring baseball player (played by actor Dennis Quaid) to give up his minor-league pitching career and abandon his lifelong ambition to play professional ball. He resorts to the next best thing: coaching a high-school team in the Texas town where he grew up and where his parents still live.

His team, noting their coach's pitching strength during practice, asks why he doesn't try out for the majors again. He responds with a defeatist attitude that mimics his father's distant and nonsupportive manner: "I've had my shot," he says, and turns away.

The team, sensing their coach's innate skill, makes a deal with him: If they win the district championship, he will try out for a major-league ball club. Going from worst to first, the team makes it to state, and their coach is forced to live up to his end of the deal.

Using his amazing fastball, he tries out for and makes the Tampa Bay Devil Rays organization. To top that, he ends up pitching in a major-league game as a thirty-five-year-old rookie. At the end of that game, he spots his father, who has by now painfully recognized their relational loss. A conversation ensues, resulting in reconciliation and a healing moment between the two men. "Watching you tonight—not many fathers get a chance to do that," his dad says. "I guess I let too many of those things get away." The dad realized a valuable lesson: while it is impossible to go back and undo past mistakes, we can still make significant decisions for today.

Whether we're twenty-five or sixty-five, we can choose daily to invest in our key relationships.

Kristen's Perspective

I asked my collaborative writer, Warren Bird, to interview my children. He asked them what they felt their priority actually was in Carolyn's and my daily schedule, what values they inherited, and what contradictions they saw between our ideals and those values. They both took the challenge seriously, asking for several days to collect their thoughts.

Kristen, age twenty-six at the time of this writing, says, "I always felt my brother and I were top priority with our parents." She remembers them letting her miss school in fifth grade so she could go on a business trip with her dad to San Francisco and Monterey Bay. "They came to all my games at school when I was a cheerleader and on the soccer team," she adds.

She looked forward to the annual back-to-school ritual of going with her dad to the mall to buy an entire outfit, including shoes and jewelry. "My parents had a way of making me feel special," she says. "They would do anything for me."

The roughest years for Kristen were high school and early college. "My parents were so straight-on," she says. "I felt they were strict and ridiculous. As a teen I'd get very frustrated with them because they put restraints on me and would not budge."

"I gave them a hard time when I was in high school," she acknowledges, but she also remembers her parents' affirmations during those years. "They told my brother and me that we would do more to extend God's kingdom than they ever will."

As an adult, Kristen owns many of her parents' values for herself: "My husband and I share the importance of a relationship with God, of family, of being involved actively in a church community, and of education to better ourselves. My parents taught me that I can do whatever God wants me to do," she affirms.

She says she got her achievement focus from her dad, but her softer, more emotional side from her mom. "I have high expectations of other people, and that is something I 'caught' from my dad," she says. "But sometimes my parents' high expectations of me clashed with me wanting to be my own person, and it adversely affected our relationship for a few years." The relationship was rebuilt through "prayer on their part and a life-changing decision I made on a mission trip," she explains.

"I'm really thankful for how it turned out," she says. "Had my parents not done all they did—the dad-daughter dates, the special gifts, and investments of time and energy, things they didn't have to do—I don't know how things would have turned out. My parents were real. My mom is my closest friend now," Kristen says.

Jonathan's Point of View

Jonathan, three years younger, shares many of Kristen's evaluations. "They put God first, and then family close behind," he says. "They don't just talk about it; they model it. We saw them having devotional time with God in the mornings; they took us to church even when we didn't want to go; and they were always there for our school functions."

"We were a high priority—my Mom gave up her job to raise us kids," says Jonathan, who is quick to identify positive values that he gained from his parents. "From both of them I learned to do things with a 110 percent effort. From Mom, I got my sense of compassion and service, and from Dad I learned how to become a better leader. 'That's not how a leader would act,' my Dad would say, and then he'd coach me on how to do it differently."

Jonathan even sees some of the multigenerational transfers that have taken place. "My dad inherited an intensity from his mother that stays stuck on something until it gets done. That trait developed a perfectionism in me: When I'm a leader, I want it done right the first time, and done with excellence—never settling for less than the best."

Sometimes his dad's intensity has led to friction between father and son. "It's hard for Dad to let something drop—something he feels I should or should not do," Jonathan says. A few years ago, Jonathan had to decide whether to spend a second year with Athletes in Action or take on a different challenge, such as joining Teach for America, which positions promising leaders in underresourced public schools. "My dad had a strong view," Jonathan says. "Mom had to say, 'Let Jonathan make the decision.'" In the end, Jonathan chose teaching, and he says he trusted God as he worked through that decision, just as his parents had taught him to do.

The intensity trait works the other way too. "I got my Dad to promise that we'd get matching tattoos," says Jonathan, and he pushed his father for four years until it happened. "I had to take the initiative. It was my ambition more than his, so maybe it got pushed back a bit on my dad's priorities." Both chose to have an ancient Christian symbol tattooed on their right shoulders to make the statement of who and Whose they are.

Occasional raised voices and head-butting aside, Jonathan appreciates his parents' style. "Their yes is yes, and no is no," he says. "So when Dad says, 'Trust me on this one,' I often do."

Jonathan saw a model in his parents that he affirms for others. "If you don't put your family just behind God as a priority, and you're not investing in the daily life of your kids, I don't see why adults should get mad if their children aren't close to them when they grow up, or if they don't accept their parents' values. It takes relationship to transfer values between parent and child."

The People in Your Scope

The second mentoring responsibility we have is with the people in our scope—those strategic to God's mission in our network of influence. All people are equally important to God, but all people are not equally strategic to the investment of our time for God's mission. Jesus ministered to the multitudes, but he strategically spent the majority of his time mentoring his twelve disciples. The ultimate test of success is not what we accomplish or achieve but whom we develop.

All of us must be strategic when it comes to the time we spend with people. As a pastor I learned early on to mark my calendar with strategic think time and strategic people time. It may take two or three weeks for some people to get an appointment to meet with me. I must be a good steward of the time that God has given me, and I must name my own priorities.

You make an impact in the world by making a difference in the lives of other people. It is too easy to become distracted by the wrong priorities. Pastors begin to focus on building programs. Businesspeople pour their energy into building companies. Teachers turn their attention to building lesson plans.

Whatever your type of work, the priority is building people. The ancient Jewish worshipers sang this value as they linked the measure of their work to its influence on people: "May you see the prosperity of Jerusalem; . . . [and] may you live to see your children's children" (Ps. 128:5-6). The call of Jesus is a call to make time outside our homes and jobs for a greater purpose in the world—investing in God's mission through the lives of people.

When I look at where I am and what I've accomplished in life, I envision a circle of people who are standing around me. They are the teachers, coaches, youth mentors, professors, businesspeople, and others who supported Carolyn and me when we made the choice to go into ministry. They are all surrounding us with words of encouragement, reminding us to be faithful in finishing the race well.

Now it's my turn to stand behind others—the people in my scope.

Strategic Investments

I regularly set aside time to meet with Mike Berry, a pastor I am mentoring as the leader of Medway United Methodist Church, a congregation twenty miles east of Ginghamsburg Church. Our bishop was planning to close this aging, dying church, and he asked us if we'd take it under our wing and take one last shot at redeveloping it.

God raised up Mike, who had been part of Ginghamsburg. As a civil engineer, Mike had no formal seminary education, but he sensed God's call to invest himself as pastor of this church. What's happening at Medway Church has been nothing short of resurrection—a resurrection that mimics Mike's own conversion.

Fourteen years ago Mike stopped drinking, but a lot of things in his life didn't improve. "I was a recovering alcoholic, and I was taking out my unhappiness on anyone who got in my way, including my dog," he says. His wife, Tracy, had moved out and taken their two children with her. In one last-ditch attempt, they decided to try church before resorting to divorce. "Why don't we see if God will do a miracle?" Tracy suggested.

"We came to church and something happened about ten minutes into the sermon," says Mike. "The Holy Spirit got hold of us, and things have never been the same."

Mike and Tracy rebuilt their marriage around God. "We have grown together, we have grown in ministry, and we have been blessed because of this great God we found at Ginghamsburg Church," Mike says.

It was a seven-year journey between Mike's first visit to Ginghamsburg and what he is doing today as pastor of a United Methodist church. "My career has been in civil engineering; I can't pastor!" Mike told God when he sensed the initial call. "But through Jesus Christ I can, and I am only getting started in serving the Lord."

Mike has learned most of what he knows by being mentored through Ginghamsburg's example. "They asked me to take food to a needy family," Mike explains. "Then they asked me to pray with the family when I got there. They asked me to lead a Christian twelve-step group, and then to become a care pastor. A couple of years later, they asked me to conduct a funeral. Each time, I said, 'I can't,' but with each new experience I learned to tap into God's strength."

Mike meets regularly with me for a "Tuesday at two" mentoring session. He asks me to share experiences and ideas for reaching more people for Jesus Christ. "I usually come with a list of questions about my own walk with the Lord or about how to lead a church more effectively," Mike says.

Mike started his church appointment in October 2003, with an attendance of seventy to eighty persons. Within eighteen months it was climbing to 150. More remarkably, the age of the average attendee has dropped thirty years and the church has grown from just a handful of children to fifty during that same period. "The momentum of the church has changed from relatively flat and dead to enthusiastically mission-driven," says Mike. "Now ministry is happening every day of the week, from our food pantry to small groups meeting in homes. And I'm still putting family above ministry in my own priorities. My wife and family are located immediately after my personal relationship with Jesus."

"My greatest fulfillment," Mike says, "is that God could use a bottom-feeder like me, someone so offtrack in life, to help others become new creatures in Christ, to grow and change." (View Mike Berry's story at www.ginghamsburg.org/mflresources.)

I am thankful to be investing in this key relationship.

Identify Your Relational Investments

Who is in that invisible line of people standing behind you? Teachers, coaches, scout leaders, church leaders, campus ministers, professors, or businesspeople? Who has encouraged you, given you a break, or even supported you financially? Whose investment in your life allows you to stand where you are standing today? Who stands behind you?

And who are you standing behind? Who are you parenting, mentoring, coaching, encouraging, managing, or leading? Who is receiving the intentional, strategic time in your schedule for relationship building? The investment you are making in people today is the only one that will live beyond your lifetime, so invest wisely, reminding others to be faithful and finish well.

Rest Area Reflections

Read aloud the main Scripture, Psalm 128.

1. Think about the idea that Work + Relationship = Worship. Do you lean more toward work or relationships?

2. Describe the dinner table ritual in the home where you were raised.

3. When was the last crisis that caused you to realize you are not in control? Did you take any positive steps toward the people in your life at that time?

4. Name one person outside your immediate family whose life you are influencing toward God.

5. Are there any action steps that God is pressing on your heart? Something you need to:
   • Say to someone?
   • Schedule into your day?
   • Do as a relational investment?

CHAPTER FIVE

visioning for the future

VISION> The act of seeing or the ability to see; a picture formed in the mind; imaginative foresight; a supernatural apparition.

Our feet are standing in your gates, Jerusalem. (Ps. 122:2)

We live in a world where change is constant. Look at the major innovations that have become such integral parts of our lives during the last ten years or so. We have become so dependent on these emergent technologies for the transaction of our daily affairs that we would be immobilized without them.

- **Internet.** It is amazing how dependent I have become on the Internet. It gives me everything from instant information to the world's largest music store. I have two offices, one at home and one at the church, each containing a modest library of books. For the same price as one of those books, I can buy access for a month to a million others in libraries all over the world. Until recent years, it would have been unheard of for a person in my profession not to have a rather extensive library for the adequate preparation of sermons. Now the Internet provides almost limitless streams of information from everywhere imaginable, all while I sit in my favorite chair. The same thing happens with music. As a teen I would buy 45-rpm records for ninety-nine cents each. Now for the same money I can go to a digital jukebox called iTunes (www.itunes.com) without ever leaving my home and download my favorite songs, and the sound quality is better than on those black vinyl disks with grooves on them! I also use the Internet to pay bills, order airline tickets, buy specialized motorcycle parts at an online auction, and check my bank balances.
- **Cell phones.** Earlier I described the mission trip where Carolyn and I were teaching at a camp in the mountains of the Czech Republic. We were three hours from a major city, but we could

use our cell phones to call our children back in the United States to see how their day was going. We could take pictures on those same phones and e-mail them so our children could see what we were seeing. We also use our cell phones to play video games, log onto the Internet, or send text messages.

- **E-mail.** I am sending 90 percent less mail through the U.S. postal service and am saving a lot of money on long-distance telephone calls that I used to make and phone conferences I used to take part in. Many people at Ginghamsburg choose to receive the church's newsletter by e-mail. What an incredible savings on trees, paper, and postage! The stewardship that can be applied through the use of this technology makes resources available for the vital mission of Jesus in setting oppressed people free.
- **Portable computers and PDAs (personal digital assistants).** I have come to expect and depend on wireless Internet access wherever I am working in my travels. If I'm in a coffee shop, airport, conference facility, hotel, school, library, or church, I get frustrated when a wireless Internet connection is not available. Going wireless gives me a tremendous sense of freedom and much increased productivity.
- **Memory storage disks (CDs and DVDs).** The whole idea of recordable, portable disks brings our culture to another place. I can put a dozen translations of the Bible or the news story a local television station did about our inner-city clubhouse on one disk.
- **Digital cameras.** I can't remember when I bought my last roll of film! Several years ago I changed from the 35mm format to a digital camera. I love it. I don't have to buy film or wait for it to be developed. I get instant, high-quality results with a reusable, easily portable memory card.

If my life's work is to be an honorable, excellent offering to God, I can't ever afford to become content or comfortable staying where I am.

These changes affirm that we live in a time of exponential and revolutionary change. If my life's work is to be an honorable, excellent offering to God, I can't ever afford to become content or comfortable staying where I am.

The Power of Vision

The essence of faith is vision. "Faith is being sure of what we hope for and certain of what we do not see. This is what the ancients were commended for" (Heb. 11:1-2). These verses come from one of my favorite chapters in the Bible. Hebrews 11 defines the hallmarks of faith, showcasing people of God who are always stretching forward. They long for a better world, a heavenly one, where the peace of God rules for every person. As long as one person lacks the peace and wellness of God, the love and purpose of God compels the true follower of Jesus forward for the well-being of the planet.

Abraham could not be content with his personal wealth or the rich blessings of family that he experienced. At a ripe old age he left everything that was familiar to make a journey of ascent. "For he was looking forward to the city with foundations, whose architect and builder is God" (Heb. 11:10). Faith is looking forward, living with a forward focus. Abraham's task and ours is to work together with God for a better world; that is why we are here.

Until I came into a relationship with Jesus, life was all about me. When Jesus came into my life, I became a partner with him in reimagining God's purpose for planet Earth. We're working together, building a heavenly planet, a place where the peace of God rules for every person. If one person in the world does not have God's peace, then my call is to start another worship celebration, preach another sermon, build another relationship, or strike up another conversation.

Life isn't meant to get easier with increased age and income. My job is to be on a lifelong Psalm of Ascent. With the power of vision, I am always moving forward to become my best *in* the world and *for* the world.

Vision is the natural result of living in the fullness of the Holy Spirit. On the day of Pentecost, the Apostle Peter quoted from the prophet Joel: "In the last days, God says, I will pour out my Spirit on all people. Your sons and daughters will prophesy, your young men will see visions, your old men will dream dreams" (Acts 2:17). Through the Holy Spirit we have access to the mind of Christ, which enables us to have connection to the limitless ideas of God.

> **Through the Holy Spirit we have access to the mind of Christ, which enables us to have connection to the limitless ideas of God.**

This is why I make it a daily practice to intentionally envision God's purpose and direction for my future. Establishing a daily discipline of envisioning God's future is critical. It allows me to formulate a life picture; articulate a healthy, positive life attitude; and initiate strategic life actions.

Formulate a Picture of Life

All physical realities begin with a mental picture. Vision is about formulating, developing, and giving birth to that new reality. God's vision is developed and birthed through real followers of Jesus. Just as God birthed Earth's Savior through the available womb of a servant named Mary, God is still seeking available servants through whom miracles for the salvation of the world can be born. Every new creation begins in the mind of God. "In the beginning was the Word, and the Word was with God, and the Word was God. . . . The Word became flesh and made his dwelling among us" (John 1:1, 14 NIV). This pattern starts with creation itself. God conceived it and articulated the thought, and the Word became material reality.

The architects who designed your office, church, or home didn't start with a bulldozer. Before a shovel ever touched the ground, they saw something in their minds—pictures in detail. They articulated them through blueprints used for the actual construction. Every single piece in those buildings began with a picture in a person's mind.

The vision process works the same for you and me. You must be able to conceive an idea before you can achieve it! God wants to birth a miracle through your life's work, but you must be willing to *receive* it by submission to Jesus' authority in your life. You then have to *conceive* the big idea of God through the disciplines of daily **D**evotion and **R**eadiness for lifelong learning. As you gain skill in the practice of active listening— "Be still, and know that I am God" (Ps. 46:10)— God will *achieve* miracles through you.

The sequence is powerful: receive, conceive, and achieve. This is the process of visioning— the disciplined practice of formulating God's specific purpose for your life.

Jeremiah was an effective prophet, but before God could use him he had to formulate God's vision. The first question God asked Jeremiah was, "What do you see?" (Jer. 1:11, 13). All physical realities begin with a mental picture.

> **Visioning is the disciplined practice of formulating God's specific purpose for your life.**

88

This is why you have to be careful about the pictures you nurture, and why pornography, lust, and everything else you allow into your mind truly matter. Your thoughts become the root of your physical fruit.

People tend to live with one of two perspectives. Some have a microscopic view of life and others have a telescopic view. Which one is your primary perspective?

If you have a microscopic perspective, your perception of life is based on your current circumstances: what you see, what you feel, and what you hear in the present moment. You are focused on the immediate.

When my bishop moved me to Ginghamsburg Church, I was excited. I knew God was going to shake the world from the little hamlet of Ginghamsburg. But the first time my mother came and saw our two-room country church building with fewer than one hundred people and a $27,000 annual budget, she felt and saw something very different. To her, the only thing here was a church in a terrible location with limited facilities and people resistant to growth and change. "My, my, my," she moaned. "What have they done to my baby? You have a master's degree!"

A person with a microscopic view tends to focus on life's problems, on obstacles and limitations. Microscopic people often approach life with a scarcity mentality.

Some of Jesus' disciples did that. When he presented them with the challenge of feeding five thousand people, all they could see were problems, obstacles, and limitations. "Where are we going to get the money?" "There are too many people." "The closest food is more than an hour away." (See John 6:5-7.)

In contrast, the person with a telescopic perspective is looking forward to what God is creating in the future. Whereas microscopic people focus on problems, telescopic people see the possibilities. They have confidence that "all things are possible with God" (Mark 10:27).

The prophet Elisha had a possibility focus. He had become a thorn in the side of the king of Aram, who was seeking to destroy Israel. The king of Aram would say, "Set an ambush here," but Elisha would send a message to the king of Israel: "Watch out when you're passing this place, because Aram has set an ambush there." This kind of thing happened frequently, and the king of Aram became furious at Elisha.

The king of Aram sent out spies to discover Elisha's whereabouts. They learned that he was in a city called Dothan, or perhaps on its outskirts, so the king dispatched an impressive fighting force of horses and chariots. They came by night and surrounded the city.

Upon awakening in the morning, Elisha's servant made the grim discovery of the imminent danger. Needless to say, he had a microscopic response and was ready to run up the white flag immediately. "Oh no, my lord! What shall we do?" (2 Kings 6:15), he asked in panic.

Elisha, however, was not looking with the eyes of his head. He was seeing through the eyes of his heart, looking forward to what God was creating in the future. "Don't be afraid. . . . Those who are with us are more than those who are with them" (v. 16). What on earth was Elisha talking about? There was a sum total of two: Elisha and his servant. "And Elisha prayed, 'Open his eyes, LORD, so that he may see.' Then the LORD opened the servant's eyes, and he looked and saw the hills full of horses and chariots of fire all around Elisha" (v. 17).

The servant saw the urgency of the immediate crisis, and Elisha saw the armies of heaven.

I am a telescopic person. I didn't see a little country church building. I saw something bigger in impact than even what I see Ginghamsburg doing today. I am always looking forward to what God is creating in the future.

If I am not taking time every day to envision a better reality, I will reach my picture and retire. I can't conceive of retirement because I am constantly, every day, renewing my sense of mission by formulating a picture of what God is creating in the future. In fact, my picture is so big that sometimes I worry, "I am fifty-five; how am I going to get this done by the time I die?"

Vision can be defined as a promising picture of God's preferred future. It creates greater energy and generates bigger strategic actions. It gives energy to initiate and sustain the journey of ascent.

Vision—a promising picture of God's preferred future—gives energy to initiate and sustain the journey of ascent.

Envision a Destination

Vision is focused on the promised destination. Many parents have a common experience when taking their young children on a vacation or outing in the car. Carolyn and I would be heading to Florida on spring break. We couldn't reach the Ohio state line before our kids would say, "When are we going to get there?" and, "Are we there yet?" Most parents have heard that question a zillion times.

I remember the "Are we there yet?" experience of my childhood family's first long vacation. It was 1958, and I was seven years old. My dad had just bought a brand-new blue and white Chevy Bel Air. We were going thirteen hundred miles to my uncle's house on Key Biscayne Island near Miami. This was before the interstate highway system was up, so it took us three long days. With no air conditioning and plastic covers on the seats, my hairline hurt from the wind blowing through our open windows.

What sustained me was my uncle's description of the ocean. Before we left, he was talking to me on the telephone, telling me about the ocean and beach. I had never seen the ocean. Uncle Doc's picture of the promised destination—his description of the beach—sustained me for the three-and-a-half-day journey.

It was no doubt tempting for my parents, in light of the incessant complaints coming from my sister and me in the backseat, to stop short of their destination. Our second night was in the beautiful hills of Tennessee, a great spot for a vacation. But they had made a focused commitment to arrive at my uncle's house in Key Biscayne.

One of the early Psalms of Ascent, sung toward the beginning of the journey to Mount Zion, contained a visual reminder of the destination. The people's intention was to "go to the house of the LORD" (Ps. 122:1). What was the picture these Israelite worshipers held in their heads? "Our feet are standing in your gates, Jerusalem" (v. 2). They held onto that picture, a vision of their destination, until they got there. That is similar to the formation of your own blueprint for the realization of God's future in your life.

When I came to a small, semirural country church, I didn't picture myself as a pastor of a little church with ninety people and a $27,000 annual budget in a two-room facility on less than an acre of land. I envisioned myself as the pastor of thousands. I acted, thought, and planned as the leader of thousands. That was the picture I believed was from God.

A Growing Vision

Visioning is a daily process of formulating and refining my own life calling. After one of my times of **D**evotion in 2004, I spent some time reading about the current crisis in the Sudan. (**R**eadiness for lifelong learning demands that I read a lot and stay informed about the world. It's important for me to do ministry "with a Bible in one hand and a newspaper in the other," as theologian Karl Barth famously said.) I've been follow-ing the plight of Sudan, where a lack of food, the spread of disease, and the ongoing conflict has torn apart the lives of more than three million people, mostly children and women. The U.S. Congress has labeled the situation in Sudan as genocide. World attention is at last looking into the reports of government-backed militias, mass murder, systematic sexual violence, and the brutal slaughter of black Africans. It's being called the world's worst humanitarian crisis.

In late 1998, when the biggest known problem in Sudan was starvation from massive crop failure, God began to give me a picture of what we could do. Citing Isaiah 58, I reminded the congregation, "You have power with God by your actions toward people, espe-cially people in need." In 1999, I held up a *Dayton Daily News* photo of Sudan next to a photo ad in the same section of the paper for a new luxury sedan. Then I said, "It says 770,000 people are on the verge of death because of starvation, and I did-n't even know about it. I'm very aware of these luxury sedans, including the twelve-speaker sound system and the sixteen-position reclining seats. What bothers me is that I'm far less aware of the Sudan." Why are we well informed about the *sedan* but oblivious to starvation in the *Sudan?*

Why are we well informed about the sedan but oblivious to starvation in the Sudan?

We took action, beginning to give generously and sacrificially, wanting to live out the heart of God and the compassion of Jesus. "People are dying, and we're oblivious," I reminded our congregation. We began to wake up from our selfishness. Ginghamsburg middle-school students alone raised $4,000 to build two fresh-water wells. A congregation-wide offering on Christmas 2004 sent $312,000 to the United Methodist Committee on Relief (UMCOR), funding an agricultural development program that is assisting more than five thousand Sudanese families.

By Lent 2005, my vision had begun to spread to others, including a cell group of servants in the church who were available for God's vision to be birthed through them as well. These men and women conceived, articu-lated, and ultimately achieved an additional offering for hunger relief. The idea was for each person in our church to fast one meal a week and put the cost of that meal into an envelope. These would be collected as a special Easter offering and given toward Sudanese hunger relief. They called it "Fast for Famine." (View the story about Fast for Famine and the Sudan Miracle Offering at www.ginghamsburg.org/mflresources.)

In December 2005, our Christmas Miracle Offering raised $530,000, which we deployed in partnership with UMCOR to develop a five-year program that, in its first year, trained 152 teachers, built or rehabilitated 60 classrooms, and provided educational materials to 15,000 children. In 2006, our Christmas Miracle Offering topped one million dollars! The money took us into the second year of our five-year child protection and development program and allowed us to launch a four-year project to provide safe water and sanitation for nearly a quarter of a million people, helping meet the most critical health need in the Darfur region today.

The $1.8 million raised by Ginghamsburg's members speaks volumes about the role of self-discipline in accomplishment, influence, and leadership. We asked our members to reduce by half the amount they would spend on Christmas gifts and to donate an equal amount to our efforts in Darfur. Their living example of self-discipline and sacrifice provides a model for others as we hope to inspire an ever-growing reaction to the Sudan's ongoing crisis.

That's why I keep praying, reading, and learning about the Sudan. One morning a few years ago, I sat at the breakfast table and drew a picture for Carolyn of the orphanage that I picture our church constructing for the children in the Sudan. I saw the picture complete with a guesthouse so that we can have medical and support teams on the premises twelve months out of the year. Elsewhere there will be dormitories, classrooms, and a chapel. We will then raise scholarships for each of the children who live in the orphanage to attend Africa University, a United Methodist school.

My sketch is not a sudden, hastily assembled plan. It represents a vision that grows and is refined every day, a blueprint for the realization of God's picture. I take time every day to visualize God's promised future. I know that if my vision is fuzzy or clouded this will affect everyone I influence and am connected to. How great the cost would be if I allowed God's vision to be interrupted and ultimately omitted from the lives of those in my circle of care. We must faithfully receive, conceive, and work to achieve the picture of God's promised destination.

Vision is a contagious commodity, by the way. It can captivate a church of any size. The pastor of a church of one hundred people came to one of our conferences and was inspired by what we were doing in the Sudan. He went back and led his church to make a miracle offering of more than $7,000 for the Sudan.

Another person, from a church of two hundred, went home from a different Ginghamsburg conference convicted of her personal need to be financially free so that she could better respond to others in need. "One theme kept jumping out at me, which at first I tried in vain to ignore and suppress," she wrote us. "It was the issue of financial health—tithing and being debt-free. . . . As you talked about our responsibility as Christians to not allow mediocrity in any area of our lives, I came to tears as I felt God right beside me, encouraging me to let go of this one area of my life in which I'd not yet allowed Him to be Master and to trust Him with my whole life. . . . In my heart I yielded completely to God and promised to act immediately to bring true health to my financial situation." She then drove back to her hometown. Even before she went to her house, she met with a friend from church who helped her take steps to bring her financial situation under control.

As John Wesley repeatedly told his followers, "Catch on fire for God and people will come and watch you burn!" Vision pulls us upward to bolder life actions. When you and I are dreaming God-size dreams, we don't have the time to contemplate retirement. I figure I need to live to age 127 to accomplish all the plans that God is igniting in my heart. People retire because they get tired of doing the same old things, but God creates new wine that makes our life's work and creations new every morning!

> **Vision pulls us upward to bolder life actions.**

Persevering toward the Future

Vision also inspires perseverance. After Moses' death, Joshua accepted the call and challenge to lead God's people into the land of promise. "I will give you every place where you set your foot, as I promised Moses" (Josh. 1:3). After making this promise to Joshua, God then provided a more detailed blueprint for a vast expanse of territory that extended from the Euphrates River in the east to the Mediterranean Sea in the west (see Josh. 1:4).

God's promise was a done deal. All Joshua and the people of God had to do was keep on stepping forward. The verses that follow exhort Joshua, in effect, "Don't stop, look back, or deviate to the left or the right. In the face of opposition and conflict, just keep on keeping on. Stay on the journey of ascent. Don't become comfortable or satisfied when you begin to be filled with fruits that are produced in the land of milk and honey. The abundance you experience today is not yet the place of ultimate promise. The resistance you meet tomorrow is not the place of ultimate defeat. Don't quit, stop, or settle for anything less than the realization of the place of promised destination that you visualized when you first heard God call your name."

A good friend who has been closely acquainted with my ministry regularly reminds me of my ordinary-ness. "Mike, if I look at any one of your twenty-eight years here—no matter which one I pick—I can't point to any one year that you've done anything really great. . . . The thing is, you just don't go away!"

My friend is right. I just keep walking toward the vision God gave me when I came here in April 1979. At that time I was very concerned with discovering God's mission for the church. I knew this little country church had been in existence since 1863. I also knew that each of the people involved would have opinions. At twenty-seven years of age, I sensed that my life and ministry were too short to be about anything less than the purpose of God. So I established, as my first priority, the ability to "see" God's purpose.

As I tell the story in my first book, *Spiritual Entrepreneurs*:

> On a chilly but sunny April morning, I went and stood in a field behind the little two-room church building—the site of our current counseling center. Staring back at the modest church facility that looked like hundreds of others, I said: "Lord, I am not going to leave this field until I have a clear sense of your mission for this church."
>
> I remained in the field for the rest of the afternoon. And as is so often the case, God speaks, not through storm, fire, or earthquake, but through silence. God's thoughts began to stream into my head. I could see three thousand people worshiping the Lord. A deep sense of God's feeling for the lost overwhelmed me. I am not a highly emotional person, but tears ran down my cheeks as I sensed God's pain for the people who lived thirty minutes in every direction from this location—people who had no understanding of God's love and healing intention.
>
> I had a vision of a church that would be a teaching church, a place where ordinary people would come and be equipped to be fully assimilated and functioning members of the Body of Christ—disciples who would go out into the marketplace and win the lost; followers of Jesus who would be committed to work in the inner city in ministries to help set free the oppressed; people of compassion who would do lay counseling and develop support-group ministries. A picture of pastors and lay people coming to this place from other churches was forming in my

spirit. They would come here to see what God was doing and take what they learned back to other churches, throughout our denomination and beyond, promoting renewal.

I also saw a church that represented ethnic diversity, where the songs of all cultures were sung and celebrated.

When I left the field it was late afternoon. I left with a sunburn and a clear sense of God's purpose, which has kept me moving forward and sustained me during my ministry at Ginghamsburg Church. This experience has been the basis for everything that has taken place. The power of vision enabled me to see the reality of God's success before it happened.

When a leader has a clear picture of God's destination, the people begin to articulate and live that vision. Over a period of time, that vision begins to penetrate the surrounding culture. . . . Vision clarifies God's purpose and direction.[1]

Too many pastors and other leaders leave their church or place of employment in the face of resistance and opposition. They never experience the promise of God because they quit stepping forward; they start over again back at the beginning.

You will never reach God's place of promise if you keep starting over. Many people do this not only in their life's work but also in their relationships. I was headed that way when I nearly gave up on my marriage to Carolyn. We were at the twenty-year mark and frustrated by feelings of pain and failure. I am so thankful that we didn't make our decision on the basis of what we were seeing, feeling, and hearing at that moment. We chose instead to focus on what God was intending and creating for our relationship in the future. We began to build daily on the promising picture of God's preferred future. As of this writing we are celebrating more than thirty-five years of marriage and are allowing God to use our lives as a source of health and blessing for others.

Nurtured in Community

Vision is nurtured in community. The Psalms of Ascent were sung in community. You cannot climb the incline of faith by yourself. As you and I travel together on this journey, we hear each other's words and stories of faith.

Steve is a physician in our church who leads medical mission teams several times a year to locations all over the world. After a recent trip he was sharing with me how $40,000 a year would support an orphanage of three hundred children in a third-world country. That statement triggered my vision. I began to dream about how we as a local church could build and support schools and orphanages all around the world. What if we could get all the United Methodist churches in my *annual conference* to support this project? What if we could get every United Methodist in the *state* to give an amount equal to what they spend on Christmas toward world hunger and oppression? What if every Christian in the *country* would . . . ? What if every Christian in the *world* would . . . ? The vision began to stir because I heard Steve's song of ascent as we were together.

We cannot make this journey alone. We cannot carry ourselves to the place of wholeness or to the fulfillment of our intended destinies.

I admire the story in Mark 2:1-11 where the four men carry their paralyzed friend to Jesus. They were faithful, persistent, innovative, and resourceful. That's a rather creative group! Think about the energy it would take to get this one person, dead weight, up onto a roof and then to cut through the roof to get him down again, into the healer's care.

Notice that it took four people to bring this man to Jesus. Have you discovered that you can't get there by yourself? I appreciate this saying, "People don't go to heaven by themselves; we go in groups." Like the paralyzed man, you need someone to carry you. Carolyn and I would have never made it without others around us to bring us to healing in our relationship, nor would I have stayed at Ginghamsburg without others to help me along.

Some people come to church and say to themselves, "I can hang out by myself, come here, be inspired every weekend, and that's good enough." It's not. You need help to find Jesus through the crowd. You need the faith of your friends when your own faith falters. The paralyzed man was healed "when Jesus saw their faith" (v. 5). Whose faith did Jesus see? The faith of the man's friends.

You need the faith of your friends when your own faith falters.

Sometimes I want to ask, "God, where are you?" Do you ever feel that way? I've even found myself occasionally saying, "Is this Jesus thing for real?" We have more faith together than we do by ourselves; sometimes when it's too hard for me to trust God, other people can trust for me.

Leland, a ninety-four-year-old friend of mine, helps lower friends through rooftops to be touched by Jesus. "If I sit down at the donut shop and I don't know the person next to me, I strike up a conversation," Leland says. "Where do you go to church?" he asks them. If they say they don't go anywhere, Leland takes it as his signal to go after them. "I would say eighteen to twenty have been fetched in by my invitation," Leland reports. He doesn't just invite. He picks them up in his car and brings them to church. "At ninety-four, I won't be around here much longer," he explains, "so I want to cover as much territory in this spiritual aspect as I can. We're told that one of the things we are to do is to be about Jesus' business. So as long as I'm able, I'll be contacting individuals about their spiritual status." (View Leland's story at www.ginghamsburg.org/mflresources.)

People like Leland get involved. They're resourceful. Since the men could not get their paralyzed friend to Jesus through normal means, they made an opening in the roof above Jesus. In other words, they made doors where there were no doors. After they carved through the roof, can you imagine the mess? I can hear the synagogue people below: "We just put the roof on this building last year!" Jesus didn't die for shingles and nails; he died for paralyzed people who depend on the vision of others to bring them into the community of care and transformation.

Who are your traveling companions? Are you being pulled forward by the collective vision of those in your faith community? Each of us is responsible for developing our own networks of mentoring relationships. Vision is nurtured in community—prophetic communities that bring people to Jesus, people who then grow in authentic relationships and become empowered to serve.

Articulate an Attitude of Determined Faith

The tongue is a powerful force that has the potential to bring life or death. "A word out of your mouth may seem of no account, but it can accomplish nearly anything—or destroy it!" (James 3:5 The Message). Our words emerge from our attitudes to create physical realities. That's why the songs we sing amid the rigors of the journey are songs of celebration, faith, and victory. "If the LORD had not been on our side / . . . the flood would have engulfed us, / the torrent would have swept over us, / the raging waters would have swept us away. / Praise be to the LORD" (Ps. 124:1, 4-6).

Vision empowers me to sing songs of faith in the face of discouragement and resistance. When you grasp God's vision for your life's work, you celebrate what is right with life. You focus on the positive redemptive activity of God that is going on continually all around us. When you celebrate the good, you build vision for God's possibilities and you find energy to fix what's wrong!

We speak faith and hope on the basis of God's promise and not out of the circumstances of the moment. We demonstrate faith in the action of trust. When Peter, crossing the Sea of Galilee in a terrifying storm, heard the voice of Jesus, seemingly coming from an uncertain apparition on the water, he took an irrational risk and stepped out of the boat to attempt the impossible. " 'Lord, if it's you,' Peter replied, 'tell me to come to you on the water' " (Matt. 14:28).

Our verbal attitudes fortify trust. The ancient Jewish pilgrims affirmed that they would trust God regardless of their current circumstances, singing confidence and joy in their Psalms of Ascent: "Those who trust in the LORD are like Mount Zion, / which cannot be shaken but endures forever" (Ps. 125:1). "Our mouths were filled with laughter, / our tongues with songs of joy" (Ps. 126:2). Regardless of how the earth moves, vision allows us to have positive, healthy attitudes. People of vision trust God's promise. They are heading not toward defeat but toward victory, surplus, and abundance. One vision-challenged person in our congregation said to me, "Mike, what we are doing in the Sudan is like throwing our resources down an empty pit." I couldn't disagree more. God is preparing a banquet for the life of the world. He takes the meager offering of stale bread and a few fish and multiplies it abundantly that all might eat and be satisfied.

The Lord is on our side, affirms Psalm 124:1, and if we look ahead to the back of the book, we know God wins in the end. Jesus died on the cross and rose from the grave. The victory is final. Jesus' salvation is offered to every single person on planet Earth. I might not see the realization of it today, but as long as I am going to die anyway, I am going to sow my life toward God's future.

When I came to this little country church, I kept telling stories of what God was going to do in the future. I didn't focus on the inadequate building, the backwoods location, the meager resources, or the resistance to growth and change. Jesus did not die so that God's mission would fail. And so I keep speaking the promising picture of God's preferred future in spite of the negativity or resistance I might experience in the heat of the moment. As the pilgrims ascending to the temple long ago sang, "They have greatly oppressed me from my youth, / but they have not gained the

People of vision articulate an attitude of determined faith in all they do.

victory over me" (Ps. 129:2). People of vision articulate an attitude of determined faith in all they do.

Initiate Strategic Actions

Vision empowers us to initiate strategic actions that result in a picture of a better future. Without it, we too often reach a plateau and grow discouraged. Walt Kallestad and Kirbyjon Caldwell, in their book *Entrepreneurial Faith*, say, "One of the main causes of burnout among pastors and other leaders is that they don't execute their visions. They spend all their time and energy dancing around worn-out systems—sacred cows—and never see their vision fulfilled. After awhile, they simply give up."[2] So often, people suffering from depression and hopelessness are really plagued with a lack of vision. They cannot imagine a positive future or envision a worthy aim to which to devote their lives.

God entrusts vision to those who will faithfully execute it, and the size of vision God gives us is dependent on our faithfulness in implementing strategic action.

Ginghamsburg's approach to Fast for Famine started in a cell group in our church. They had participated in the Ginghamsburg Christmas offering for Sudan, and they wanted to do something that would keep the momentum going all year long. They couldn't shake the idea that 800 million people around the world go hungry each day. They calculated that if everyone who voted in the last presidential election gave up one meal, it would equate to $400 million.

"I was sitting down one day, thinking about what we could do and what a shame it is that so many people are without even one basic meal a day," says Ron, initiator of the idea. "All of a sudden this voice came into my head and said, 'I want *you* to do it.' I replied out loud, 'What?' But as I began to see each person plugging in at different levels, I immediately saw a part that I could play."

There are enough resources today to feed the world, and America, the world's largest food exporter, could take the lead.[3] So why can't we do something so that the people of Sudan can grow enough food? Why can't we do something to help hungry people here at home? God wants to do incredible things, but he will not give you a vision that exceeds the size of the faith-steps that you are willing to take.

God has given us everything we need according to his riches in Christ Jesus our Lord. Vision empowers us to initiate life-changing action, and God will not trust us with a bigger vision than we are willing to implement. God wants to accomplish much on planet Earth, but he is looking for people who will faithfully act on whatever ideas he places in their minds, in spite of their fear or reservations.

God is looking for people who will faithfully act on whatever ideas he places in their minds, in spite of their fear or reservations.

God gives big visions to people who are willing to take big actions! Influence and accomplishment are not about doing the same old things passed along by the managers of sacred traditions who have preceded you. Leadership implements the risky strategic actions necessary to reach God's place of promise. Doers are driven by visions and dreams and not by the expectations or reprisals of people. They are compelled forward by truth, not motivated by the accolades of committees. Leaders do the right thing rather than the expected thing.

A Strategic Action Plan

Every year I work from a strategic action plan. All the business models that present the need for vision statements, mission statements, purpose statements, and highly detailed plans confuse me. For me it's simple. I get a clear vision, and I spell out the strategic actions that I will implement this year to get closer to God's place of promise.

This is far more important than a wish list. It is not just an idea ("I'd like to do something big for God"), and it is more than a strategic goal ("I'll need to look into beginning a new worship celebration sometime soon"). It does no good if it is never executed. That is why I work from a yearly strategic action plan. For example, my one-year strategic plan for 2005 had a three-pronged focus: to start a Saturday evening worship celebration for people in recovery by Easter; to define and implement phase two of our Sudan initiative by October; and to assure the inception of one hundred new cell groups by December 31. I continue to work and plan as if I have one year to live. I call it my one-year rule. This approach allows me to prioritize on the basis of mission-critical-strategic activities. More important, it gives me permission not to do things of less importance.

A few years ago our church was gearing up to plan a new, $10 million sanctuary that would seat three thousand people. Then I asked myself the question, "If I have just one year to live, would I spend it building a worship center?" My conclusion felt right: "I don't want to spend this precious time building facilities; I want to build people." Research tells us that the postmodern generation doesn't relate to the mega-mall worship structures built by the boomer generation. They prefer smaller, more intimate venues. My new slogan became, "Minimize brick, maximize mission."

That same one-year strategic focus helped Carolyn and me in our decision to move to Philadelphia for Jonathan's senior year baseball season. We named it as a personal strategic action plan.

Vision is a core element of D-R-I-V-E because it is the motivator for self-leadership. Self-leadership in our devotional, intellectual, interpersonal, and physical lives empowers us to make our visions a reality. Notice how the self-leadership elements of D-R-I-V-E factor into the following four areas to consider in your yearly strategic action plan:

1. Total Health. If I am not healthy spiritually, emotionally, and physically, then I can't be a source of health and hope to those around me. I place self-health activities into my daily schedule, including both my devotion time and my time for exercise. Sitting down to a healthy dinner may require a specific strategic action because it requires more time and energy than simply running through a fast-food drive-thru. Being intentional about these activities requires strategic planning so that your total health is not compromised while you pursue the visions God has given you.

2. Relationships. We are created for relationships, and relationships are cultivated in the margins of our lives—the space we preserve outside of our daily tasks. I strategically make my family a priority as I plan my strategic direction for each week, month, and year. Consider the amount of time and energy you need to devote to those key people in your life, and what sacrifices may need to be made so that those important relationships can be nurtured.

3. Work. Our work is an act of worship. If my work is to continue on the upward ascent as an honorable, excellent offering to God, then I need to be growing in my daily execution. Strategic actions for your work may include a discipline of reading a weekly trade magazine, taking a continuing-education course, or leading a group of innovative thinkers. If we do not strategize about our work, it is terribly easy to get stuck in the rut of doing things in the same old ways and recycling the same tired, stagnant, or burned-out workers.

4. Mission. God holds each of us accountable for a personal mission outside of our families and workplace. Mission is a vision of a better world, put into action. You might make a strategic action plan to reprioritize your finances so that you may give more to hunger relief programs. Strategic actions for a church's mission to win the lost and set the oppressed free might include plans to start a scouting or youth sports program, a food pantry, homeless shelter, or tutoring program. These missional programs cannot function apart from a strategic commitment to sacrificial service.

Part of my strategic action plan for mission involves working with a group of young college and postgraduate students to help them become the radical, excellent Christian leaders of their generation. We meet periodically in different parts of the country for leadership-learning experiences. I assign them regular reading, and I am raising a young hero scholarship fund for any of these young people who pursue graduate work for the purpose of vocational ministry. This personal mission strategy is separate from my home or work commitments, but is a crucial part of the vision God has given me.

A great strategic plan will focus on a few well-defined and articulated initiatives. Most people try to do too many things in any one year. When it came to my one-year strategic action plan for my first year at Ginghamsburg Church, I did three things.

First, I preached a sermon series from the book of Acts. This was offered to illustrate the true purpose and mission of the church. As Rick Warren says in the first sentence of *The Purpose-Driven Life*, "It's not about you." [4] We are here to serve the mission of Christ. Confusion exists in the church. Our members perceive themselves to be customers when they are to be missionaries! Every week during my first year at Ginghamsburg, I came back with a hard-hitting relevant message from the book of Acts. I challenged each person's worldview by contrasting it with the worldview of Jesus.

Second, I simplified the administrative structure to serve Christ's mission rather than the mission of serving an antiquated structure. The little country church I came to had nine boards and committees. The people were spending an average of sixteen nights a month in generally fruitless meetings that really had nothing to do with the true mission of Christ.

We now have one board of nine people who meet one night a month, ten or eleven times a year. Isn't it amazing that one "committee" can lead a church with almost five thousand in attendance each week, working in mission around the world? Yet the little church I started with had less than one hundred people but nine committees.

People are energized for the mission of Jesus when they have an opportunity to experience significance on the front lines. People are seeking a life mission, not a meeting!

Third, I poured myself into ten strategic leaders who would become the leaders of the movement. In my first three months at Ginghamsburg Church, I identified a small group of influential people who had both heart and skill. Even then I realized that all people are equally important to God, but all people are not equally strategic for the investment of my time toward God's mission.

People are seeking a life mission, not a meeting!

We met in our home one night a week and practiced the ancient art of discipleship. We read Christian classics like Dietrich Bonhoeffer's *Cost of Discipleship*. Within months these people went out and started disciple cell groups of their own and became innovative, risk-taking members of our church board. Any organization will stagnate or fail if it has people in decision-making places who are not faithfully envisioning the promised place of the future.

What strategic actions can you take that will enhance your life and work and help make God's vision for the world a reality? Life is too short to live for anything less than a fulfilling, fruitful, faithful purpose. Take time every day to dream God's dream for your life. God gives great vision to those who are willing to take great action!

Rest Area Reflections

Read aloud the main Scripture, Psalm 122.

1. Were you raised to be a microscopic person or a telescopic person?

2. Who is/are the person(s) that help(s) nurture your vision?

3. Celebrating what's right gives us energy to fix what's wrong. Do you naturally "speak faith" or feel compelled to say what's wrong in life situations?

4. What life-picture is God showing you that you would like to begin putting into action?

5. Do you know the strategic action steps you must take, or do you need to connect with a strategic partner to help design a plan? What is your next step?

CHAPTER SIX

eating and exercise for life

EAT> To consume as sustenance; to include something as a usual or fundamental part of a diet.

EXERCISE> To exert oneself physically or mentally, especially for the purpose of developing or maintaining physical fitness.

*May the LORD bless you from Zion;
may you see the prosperity of Jerusalem
all the days of your life.
May you live to see your children's children—
peace be on Israel. (Ps. 128:5-6)*

Have you ever heard someone make a statement like, "I can't wait to go to heaven" or "I hope that Jesus is coming back soon"? Personally, I can wait! I am in no hurry to make the celestial trip. It's not that I won't be happy to see Jesus—I'm just really enjoying this incredible gift of life.

Sometimes we tend to be like the spoiled child who rips eagerly through the wrapping on Christmas morning but grows bored with the present and discards it by late afternoon. Life is a gift to be embraced and celebrated to the max. I love life's complexities and its intricacies as well as its ordinary joys. I look forward to my first cup of coffee each morning. I look forward each fall to the first snow. In fact, each of the four seasons continues to bring me a new sense of wonder.

Even the simple day-to-day routines of life add sparkle to my world. I find richness in pitching baseballs to my son or hearing the enthusiasm in my daughter's voice when she calls and says, "Hi, Dad! How are you doing?"

107

I love marriage, work, food, family, meeting new people, and the experience of traveling the world. I love life, and I am in no hurry to let go of this precious gift.

The Gift of Life

What makes life unique? The breath of God. "Then the LORD God formed a man from the dust of the ground and breathed into his nostrils the breath of life, and the man became a living being" (Gen. 2:7). The Hebrew name for Adam sounds like the Hebrew name for dirt. All the elements in a human body can be found in dirt, but you are more than the sum total of chemicals and minerals found in the natural world or elements charted on the periodic table. God breathed Spirit into the human form, adding a sense of mystery to the essence of human life.

What makes life unique? The breath of God. . . . That's why every human being matters to God.

That's why every human being matters to God. That's why Ginghamsburg Church is involved with the Sudan crisis, as millions face the threat of starvation: every single life matters! That's why I personally struggle with the issues of abortion, euthanasia, capital punishment, and war. There are no disposable people. Every human contains the breath of God that brings life. In God's eyes, every single life has value.

I heard former *Superman* actor Christopher Reeve lecture in Philadelphia in the spring of 2004, just a few months before his death. Unable even to move his head, he was totally dependent on a respirator to deliver his breath. His assistant rolled him onto the stage in an elaborate wheelchair. Yet he continued to maximize his gift of life in spite of his overwhelming physical limitations and his life-threatening injuries.

This is in stark contrast to the Clint Eastwood movie *Million Dollar Baby*, which was a big success both at the box office and at the 2005 Academy Awards. Eastwood's character turned to euthanasia when the boxer (played by Hilary Swank) experienced the same paralyzing injury as Reeve had in real life. Christopher Reeve demonstrated that the quality and value of life is not tied to the absence of debilitating injuries or disease. His life gave me fresh appreciation for the breath of God.

As a follower of Jesus Christ, no matter what your ability or disability, your body is the dwelling place of God! "Do you not know that your bodies are temples of the Holy Spirit, who is in you, whom you have received from God? You are not your own; you were bought with a price. Therefore honor God with your bodies" (1 Cor. 6:19-20).

It is tempting for us to dissociate what we eat and whether we exercise from our commitments to God, but our bodies are not our own. We have been purchased, body-mind-spirit, with the redemptive work of God through Jesus' life, death, and resurrection. Eating healthy foods and making a disciplined commitment to exercise is not optional for the committed follower of Jesus. It is one of the essential daily life *disciplines* of discipleship. "Therefore, I urge you, brothers and sisters, in view of God's mercy, to offer your bodies as a living sacrifice, holy and pleasing to God—this is true worship" (Rom. 12:1). "Let us purify ourselves from everything that contaminates body and spirit, perfecting holiness out of reverence for God" (2 Cor. 7:1).

> **Eating healthy and making a disciplined commitment to exercise is not optional for the committed follower of Jesus.**

I am amazed at how it is almost impossible to find anything in popular Christian literature about the disciplines associated with eating and exercise. I do find material on fasting from time to time, but it is rarely linked to the purpose of physical health. Yet, starting with God's instruction to the Israelites, the Bible has much to say about diet. The Bible is filled with references to the purity of the body in ways that extend beyond our sexual morality. Even so, the sin of gluttony—habitual eating to excess—seems to be the acceptable sin for much of the church, clergy, and laity alike. All references to gluttony in the Bible are negative.

We were bought with a price—the life and death of Jesus on the cross. God owns our bodies, so we must honor God in their care. Otherwise we cannot continue God's work in the excellence of ascent. God intends for the Holy Spirit to operate through my physical body. If God is going to feed dying children in the Sudan, he needs the longevity of my life and assets! The church is the hands, feet, and mouth of Jesus on planet Earth for reaching the lost and setting oppressed people free. God needs our bodies to complete the mission of Jesus in the world.

Salvation is a lifestyle of (w)holiness. The purpose of Jesus coming into our lives is not only to save us for heaven, but also to heal us and make us well in every dimension of life so that our bodies can be honorable, excellent offerings to God. Our longevity has value for Jesus' mission!

> **Salvation is a lifestyle of (w)holiness.**

I've sometimes needed to borrow someone else's larger vehicle to get my kids back and forth to college. I've noticed that when I do so, I tend to be more careful. There is almost a holy uneasiness in me during the several days it takes to go back and forth to the East Coast to move our children. In my car, if I spill a little coffee it might get cleaned up next year, but not in someone else's! The same principle applies to clutter that accumulates on the floor of my car. When I borrow someone else's, I might have it for two days, but I take the floor mats out and brush them off because I am more careful with someone else's property than I am with my own. I have a different kind of respect, one that is in keeping with what the Bible says about our bodies. Our bodies are for the Lord, and we can no longer be indifferent about our physical condition.

The Value of Longevity

The Psalms of Ascent place value on longevity. "May the LORD bless you from Zion; / may you see the prosperity of Jerusalem / all the days of your life. / May you live to see your children's children—peace be on Israel" (Ps. 128:5-6).

Your life is a gift from God. You live to serve God's purpose. The fruitful completion of that purpose and the enjoyment of the fruits of your life's labors are both best served by your continued good health. Why are our fifties, sixties, and seventies called our prime-time years? When you are healthy, you can still enjoy the energy of youthfulness, the wisdom of age, and the fruit of your accumulated years of labor.

Your time of death is not predetermined. It is affected by your life practices and choices. Somehow we don't believe that, or we wouldn't hear so many stupid statements at funerals. "I guess it was just their time to go." Come on! The person who died sped the process by smoking three packs of cigarettes a day and being seventy pounds overweight!

There is evidence from new research suggesting that long life is the result of disciplined life choices. *Time* magazine's cover article, "How to

Live to Be 100," says that the dominant factor is lifestyle rather than genetic makeup. "You could have Mercedes-Benz genes," says Dr. Bradley Willcox, of the Pacific Health Research Institute in Honolulu, "but if you never change the oil, you are not going to last as long as a Ford Escort that you take good care of."[1] The article cites studies showing that Seventh-day Adventists, who avoid alcohol, caffeine, and tobacco, tend to live an average eight years longer than other Americans.[2] There is no question that a change in eating habits and physical exercise can prolong our lives and foster greater health and vitality into our seventies, eighties, and beyond.

Obesity is one of the leading causes of preventable death in the United States. Being extremely overweight is indisputably lethal, according to the Centers for Disease Control and Prevention.[3] From 1991 to 2000, the percentage of obese Americans increased by 61 percent.[4]

Diet programs abound, but do people stay with them long enough to see lasting benefit? From Atkins to South Beach, Americans are forking over millions in hopes of finding a magic elixir while they continue to pack on the pounds. One calculation says that a third of Americans are not just overweight but obese.[5]

Obesity is also reaching epidemic proportions among our children! It tripled among seven- to fifteen-year-olds between 1985 and 1995.[6]

Cancer is also linked to our life choices. "Tobacco use, poor diet, and inadequate physical activity combined are related to about 60 percent of all cancer cases, while environmental cancer risks are related to only about 3 percent of cancer cases," reports Dr. J. Nick Baird, director of the Ohio Department of Health.[7] The trouble is that achieving maximum length and quality of life requires hard work and discipline.

Factors That Influence Longevity

Would you, with me, prefer to stay a bit longer on this earth? Would you like to find greater energy, joy, and fulfillment in this life? Consider these six factors:

1. Attitude. In recent years numerous scientific studies have shown a positive link between faith and longevity.[8] One study, for example, showed that people who pray during illness accelerate their recovery rate.[9]

On the other side, fuming at other drivers or stewing about the boss will shorten your life.[10] Stress has a strong, negative impact on your longevity. It makes your cells deteriorate faster. Its impact shows up on your skin and in your hair. Have you noticed how quickly a new president grays once he occupies the Oval Office? Nutrition and exercise play an important role in the management of stress, but so does your attitude.

2. Relationships. People with healthy relationships tend to live more satisfying lives. Even pets can have a positive impact on the health of those who live alone.

3. Genes. Genetics have some impact on our longevity and health, but a family history of heart disease or cancer doesn't mean we're doomed! Diet can make a difference in the fight against our genetic predispositions. For those of us who are genetically predisposed to prostate cancer, eating more soy, more fresh fruits, certain vegetables, and less saturated fat will decrease the risk.[11] Diet may also have an impact on the genes linked to heart disease, colon cancer, and Alzheimer's.[12]

4. Mental activity. Some parts of the brain will keep growing if they get enough exercise.[13] As we get older, it is important to keep learning new things and trying new activities. Games like crossword puzzles and Sudoku challenge our minds, and frequent reading and discussion of current events help us continue to learn new things, creating new pathways in our brains.

5. Exercise and **6. Diet.** The impact of these last two factors on a person's overall well-being cannot be overemphasized. No one wants the debilitation of diabetes; exercise and diet can help keep it at bay. The current number one cause of death in America is heart disease, but it is largely preventable. You can reduce the risk simply by exercising, eating well, and not smoking.

Not long ago I would go home after worship on Saturday nights, fix a big plate of nachos with all the works, and call it dinner! I was ignorant in regard to healthy nutrition. Part of my conversion process was the realization that loss of momentum can be based in lifestyle. It's why so many people become ineffective in their sixties. They are spiritually, emotionally, and physically tired, so they simply drop off the path of ascent and retire. I don't know about you, but I'm not going to take myself out of God's game because of poor eating and exercise habits.

The Responsibility of Leadership

As I have emphasized throughout this book, all leadership begins with self-leadership, and all of us are leaders in the sense that we have influence on those around us—our children, our friends, our coworkers and acquaintances. My influence as a leader comes down to the credibility of my witness to others. Do I demonstrate (w)holiness? Is the lifestyle of Jesus being revealed in my body, mind, *and* spirit? Am I, in the words of John Wesley, "going on to perfection"?[14] Am I growing continually in my fitness to serve the God whose salvation includes wellness?

It is impossible to lead others effectively if I cannot first lead myself. I must be on the ascent of health holiness if I am to be a healthy, positive, contagious force in the life of others!

> Do you not know that in a race all the runners run, but only one gets the prize? Run in such a way as to get the prize. Everyone who competes in the games goes into strict training. They do it to get a crown that will not last; but we do it to get a crown that will last forever. Therefore I do not run like someone running aimlessly; I do not fight like a boxer beating the air. No, I strike a blow to my body and make it my slave so that after I have preached to others, I myself will not be disqualified for the prize. (1 Cor. 9:24-27)

It all comes down to commitment to a rigorous daily discipline. This is why we are called disciples. Discipline is painful for the moment in which it is practiced. Many of Jesus' followers left the journey of ascent because they didn't want to pay the ongoing price of discipleship (see John 6:60-66). But those who continue on the incline of discipline will celebrate the blessings of God's promise. "No discipline seems pleasant at the time, but painful. Later on, however, it produces a harvest of righteousness and peace for those who have been trained by it" (Heb. 12:11).

Consider the temptation of Jesus in the wilderness. Satan's first attack was an attempt to get Jesus to submit his mind and spirit to his appetite. After Jesus fasted for forty days, the tempter suggested that Jesus' comfort and relief would come from food. "If

I must be on the ascent of health holiness if I am to be a healthy, positive, contagious force in the life of others.

you are the Son of God, tell this stone to become bread" (Luke 4:3). Jesus had the mental, spiritual, and emotional discipline to turn Satan down. Likewise, your ability to have discipline over your physical body is the doorway to all other disciplines in your life.

King David lost his integrity when he surrendered to his passions. Instead of leading his men in battle—where leaders are supposed to be— he succumbed to his lust for a married woman (see 2 Samuel 11:1-5). Part of what sets humans apart from all other created species is our ability to master physical discipline, to be able to live by the authority of God's word and the power of the Spirit, not the immediacy of our appetites. Until we are able to exercise discipline over our bodies through the power of the Holy Spirit, our minds and spirits will continue to be held hostage to our appetites and passions.

> *Until we are able to exercise discipline over our bodies through the power of the Holy Spirit, our minds and spirits will be held hostage to our appetites and passions.*

Everyone in America is dealing with exponential increases in the cost of health care insurance. Employers have to make painful decisions on important benefits that many of us assumed were guaranteed rights, and we must blame ourselves for some of those high costs. Many of us have driven up the price of care by our inattention to personal physical health. Ordained ministers of churches are some of the worst offenders! The West Ohio United Methodist Conference Treasurer says, "We spent more on medications for depression, cardiovascular disease, and sour stomachs than we did for conference benevolences."[15] In other words, we spend more on clergy health care than we do on mission! All leadership begins with self-leadership. You can't lead others until you can lead yourself, including the discipline of managing your physical health so as to lengthen your leadership.

Lengthening Your Leadership

Would you rather be a short-term leader or one who continues to influence others year after year? Nelson Mandela, the great South African leader, still lives a fruitful life of contribution as he nears his ninetieth birthday. He is spending most of his energies in the fight against AIDS. How does he continue to live faithfully and fruitfully well past eighty? It began with a practice at an early age. According to some reports, in the 1940s Mandela began the disciplined eating and exercise regime of an athlete. I read that he still gets up by 4:30 AM and begins an exercise routine by 5:00 AM that lasts at least an hour. He reads the daily papers over breakfast at 6:30 and then puts in a standard working day of twelve hours.

John Wesley was still riding the circuit, taking the good news by horseback to three or four places a day, into his eighties.

I had the privilege of attending Asbury Theological Seminary in the 1970s. Julian C. McPheeters, the school's second president, was in his eighties at that time. He was retired but still very active in the seminary community. When you heard him preach, heaven came down! I heard that he learned to water-ski in his seventies and that he was still doing aerobic exercise and working with weights in his eighties. He physically outpaced many of us who were still in our twenties! Howard Snyder makes memorable note of this man of God, saying, "Deeply committed to holistic evangelism, McPheeters was instrumental in the integration of nutrition, exercise, physical healing, and social justice, especially racial justice, into the Asbury Seminary curriculum."[16] Dr. McPheeters understood the concept that all leadership begins with self-leadership.

You cannot be a healthy influencer and agent of kingdom change if you are not demonstrating the reality of the kingdom of God within yourself. "You are the salt of the earth. But if the salt loses its saltiness, how can it be made salty again? It is no longer good for anything, except to be thrown out and trampled underfoot" (Matt. 5:13).

Balanced leadership also includes the responsibility of leading children. I have already mentioned the growing crisis of obesity among our children. This problem can largely be attributed to fast-food dependence, a result of busy lifestyles and single-parent or dual-career households. How many of us as parents turn to fast food after a hard day at work because it is cheap and easy? Morgan Spurlock's 2004 documentary *Super Size Me* was a wake-up call for a fast-food-dependent nation. Mr. Spurlock ate

> *You cannot be a healthy influencer and agent of kingdom change if you are not demonstrating the reality of the kingdom of God within yourself.*

nothing but McDonald's food three times a day for one month. His body began a rapid deterioration, exhibiting accelerated weight gain and dangerous increases in liver enzymes.

Fast is easy. Discipline is hard!

Another factor is the way today's children live more sedentary lifestyles. When I was a child, we played outside. "Mom, let me in!" I'd call, but I wasn't allowed to come back in. "I'm cold!" I'd whine. My mother would tell me to run around to warm up. "Mom, I'm thirsty," I'd try. She'd remind me to take a sip from the garden hose. Sometimes she'd bring us a snack like an apple—which we'd eat outside.

We weren't readily allowed back indoors. Mom's babysitter was the outdoors, not the television. When you have to play outdoors, you invent things to do. You are active. You are creative. It was a lot healthier than watching television, playing video games, and eating junk food.

If you are not comfortable letting your children play outside unsupervised, find time to go to the park together, get them involved in organized sports, or play catch and take walks together in the evening. Remember, your guidance and leadership involves helping your children learn the importance of physical health in a life of Christian service! Look for ways to take part in physical activities indoors too—pop in a workout video, find fun and challenging exercises and games, or dance together. There are plenty of ways to get started!

It blows me away that people are suing fast-food companies over their own discipline issues. We need to take responsibility for our own health by practicing self-leadership to resist foods and habits that limit our potential for lifelong effectiveness.

Beginning Point

Ready for a life of better eating and exercise? If you are like me, you have no idea where to begin, and you need a conversion-level experience to push you to a point where you actually take meaningful action. My head had listened for years to statements about the importance of healthy eating and exercise. My responses had ranged from "Some day I'll get to it" to "I know a lot of people who are worse off than me."

My rationalization proved dangerous. The dinner hour of Friday, August 18, 2000, found me in a Cincinnati restaurant celebrating a family birthday, when I suddenly felt faint. The next thing I remember, paramedics were shoving aspirin into my mouth and rushing me by ambulance to a nearby hospital. After a battery of tests in the next days, my doctor determined that the arrhythmia my heart had exhibited was not an indication of a diseased heart, but rather a huge wake-up call. My 911 experience was the culmination of lifestyle stress, too much caffeine, and a total disregard for physical conditioning in the journey of ascent. I knew I had to change if I wanted longevity in ministry, future anniversaries to celebrate with Carolyn, and the joy of grandchildren. My conversion had begun!

A few weeks after my heart scare, I shared during a weekend message how I intended to take charge of this neglected area of my life. I forecasted that I would begin a fitness program, but said I needed a trainer to show me how.

Chastity Layne Slone approached me after our final worship celebration and introduced herself as a certified trainer. She told me she would be willing to work with Carolyn and me. We talked about it at home, and a month later set up our first appointment with Chastity. Her first question, as with everyone she trains, was whether we had clearance from our physician. "Filling out a basic health-history evaluation at a fitness club is not enough," she said.

It really helped that we committed as a family to become healthy together. It is a blessing to agree to keep certain unhealthy foods out of the house. It is also encouraging to grow together with your children in this area. All five members of the extended Slaughter family (husband, wife, daughter, son-in-law, son) now work out on a regular basis and have become informed about healthy nutrition practices.

Fitness begins with a change of mind. Why am I willing to sweat and hurt? Because it's not about me. My life is not my own. "For to me, to live is Christ" (Phil. 1:21)! What's more, my life patterns will be inherited by the generations that follow me.

Fitness Starts with Good Nutrition: Triangle Leg #1

I am not particularly fond of the fad diets where you deprive yourself of certain foods for a period of time. Instead, I learned a plan of nutrition that Carolyn and I could practice for life. "Diet changes that really work must be a family decision," says Chastity. "If the family chef tries to offer two kinds of food, you'll reinforce the idea that nutritious food is weird, and it will lead to failure." (View the video "Shopping with Carolyn" at www.ginghamsburg.org/mflresources.)

Chastity should know. She started her fitness journey long before Carolyn and I wised up. She even competes in bodybuilding events and has won some titles. And she too had an accountability partner in her spouse. "I haven't always felt good about what I eat," she says. "It took an eight-year journey, but I don't crave soda pop the way I used to."

Chastity started at a specific point, as Carolyn and I did, where she determined that her eating and exercise habits would change. She then began to make a long series of firm decisions. "The biggest thing I see with failure is someone who never truly made a mind change," she says. "One of the reasons people give up is that there are so many choices for your food, and that's why the decision to change is so important."

Chastity also notes that people have a higher failure rate if they don't work with a professional who can develop a plan. This could be a certified trainer like her, or perhaps someone with training and passion in exercise science, such as a physical therapist. "Without help from someone knowledgeable," she says, "you will hit a plateau, and you'll think that's the best you're going to accomplish."

Though Chastity is a trainer who operates her own fitness center, she has emphasized diet just as much as exercise. One of the first questions she asked Carolyn and me was, "What are you eating?" She wanted to help us calculate how many calories we were taking in and what kinds of food we were eating. Some people, such as those who eat irregularly and snack a lot, need to journal in order to determine what they actually take in on a typical day.

In recent years, I've come to follow a healthy, balanced diet that is low in fat, and I have become conscious of my daily intake of carbohydrates. I'm learning to distinguish the healthier complex carbs from simple carbs that too quickly turn to sugar. I follow the simple rule, "if it's white it's not right," and opt for whole grains. This includes:

- Wild or brown rice instead of white rice
- Whole-wheat bread instead of white bread
- Yams instead of white potatoes
- Whole-wheat pasta instead of white pasta

Vegetables and fruits are a great way to take in healthy carbs, and again I've learned another general rule of thumb: "The brighter the color of the fruit and vegetable, the higher the value in vitamins and minerals."

I've started to study food packaging in order to gauge my daily intake of sugar. Many items state in bold letters that they are "0% fat"—but they are loaded with sugar. I have another simple rule: "Don't count daily calories; instead, pay attention to my intake of fats, carbohydrates, and sugar."

I stay away from dessert except on rare, planned occasions.

My eating frequency has also changed. I never used to eat breakfast, but now I realize how important that morning meal is. Breakfast kicks in your metabolism, and it is your metabolism that burns fat.

I now eat three healthy, balanced meals each day, and I supplement these meals with at least two or three smaller healthy snacks. With so many mini-meals, all nutritious, I never feel deprived.

With so many mini-meals, all nutritious, I never feel deprived.

Another Mike maxim: "Stay away from high-fat and high-sugar snack foods." (They will literally kill me!) Almonds and unsalted peanuts are some of my favorite snacks. I will also eat a granola bar or drink a protein supplement for one of my snacks, usually before or after a workout.

Protein is very important for muscle growth. Lean beef, chicken breast, turkey, and fish are excellent sources of protein that are also low in fat. Egg whites and beans are healthy sources for protein. I stay away from fried and breaded foods. I drink skim milk, and I drink plenty of water every day. For most people, depending on their physician's advice, it is a good idea to supplement their daily diet with a good multivitamin.

If I ever slip in my eating habits, Chastity reminds me that healthy nutrition is 80 percent of the equation in physical fitness. At first, all I could think about was the new foods I didn't especially like or the foods I had to give up. "I can't live without dessert," I'd think. Then I would remember why I'm making the change: it's not about my likes and food preferences, but the mission of the One I serve!

It's not about my likes and food preferences, but the mission of the One I serve!

Aerobic Exercise: Triangle Leg #2

Aerobic exercise is intentional physical movement that keeps my heart rate up for twenty to thirty minutes. The focus of aerobic exercise is cardio or heart health. It is important to do some form of cardio exercise at least three times a week. Many choose to have a daily regimen of walking.

This is good. I walk to as many places as possible and avoid elevators in favor of steps whenever possible.

Earlier I described the first time Chastity took me out to run for twenty minutes nonstop. "I've got to stop," I wheezed after just one minute that seemed like ten. "I'm going to die!"

Chastity promised me that it would get better, and it did within a matter of weeks. Today my aerobic exercise of choice is running three to four times a week on the treadmill. It's easier on my knees and is not affected by the Ohio weather.

The Christmas after we started our commitment to fitness, Carolyn and I bought each other a treadmill for about $800, and it is still serving us well after seven years. In fact, before beginning the next section, I will take a break from writing to do a thirty-minute run on the treadmill. See you later!

Resistance Training: Triangle Leg #3

I'm back after running three miles. It is hard to believe that I can physically do more in my fifties than I could when I was in my twenties.

The third part of the fitness triangle is creating resistance with weights. Your muscles are the furnace of your metabolism. Muscle burns fat twenty-four hours a day, seven days a week, even while you sleep. Aerobic exercise burns fat mainly during the time of the exercise, while the heart rate is increased.

I think of it this way: "Aerobic exercise makes for heart health while weight training increases physical strength." I try to do three cardio sessions a week and four weight-training sessions. In each of the four weight sessions, I concentrate on different parts of my body. This means I hit each major muscle area once a week.

I am not trying to look like Arnold Schwarzenegger; my goal is to maintain positive momentum for life. On Monday I concentrate on weight machines and free weights that work my chest and back muscles. On Tuesday morning I will do a half-hour of cardio exercise on the treadmill. On Wednesday afternoon I come back to resistance training, concentrating on leg exercises. On Thursday morning I am back to cardio, running twenty-five to thirty minutes on the treadmill. On Friday morning I spend twenty-two to twenty-five minutes on the treadmill in my basement and then hit the gym on the way home from the office in order to work my shoulder muscles (thus a double session on Friday). On Saturday morning I am back at the gym to work my triceps and biceps. Sunday is my day of rest.

Notice that I do three cardio and four weight training sessions that target all of my major muscle groups. The best way to learn to exercise with a safe, healthy routine is to become part of a gym or YMCA where they have classes and trainers who know what they are doing and can teach you to use the right form that will minimize the possibility of injury and maximize the effectiveness of your time spent in the gym.

Good nutrition is 80 percent of the key to your desired results because food is the fuel that runs the car. My body was not designed to run on inferior fuel!

> *Good nutrition is 80 percent of the key to your desired results.*

Conversion Time

Rob, a pastor in his early thirties, began visiting Ginghamsburg's website each week, going especially to the online sermons. In January and February 2002, I did a multiple-week series on D-R-I-V-E, which he saw in video stream.

"This message really spoke to me," he told us, "because in December 2003 my blood pressure went so high I had to be rushed to the emergency room. They thought I was going to have a stroke. I was diagnosed with fatty liver, high cholesterol, and high triglycerides. I was a walking, talking stroke or heart attack waiting to happen."

Rob was thirty-one years old, but you wouldn't guess it. "At my highest point, I got up to about 292 pounds," he confessed to us. "My asthma was starting to affect my ability to preach three services. I couldn't stay awake. I was mad all the time. I lost a lot of self-esteem. When I went to places all I could think about was how people were looking at me and thinking about how fat I was."

Rob began to deal with the issue that his body is a temple of the Holy Spirit. He felt that God was speaking to him and saying, "You need to get your health under control." Rob had a conversion.

He sensed that God was saying, "Rob, if you do this, you are going to lose weight." Today he exercises anywhere from thirty minutes to an hour-and-a-half, depending upon the day and the intensity of the workout. His back pains, developed because of weight gain, have lessened. He's had accountability help from Weight Watchers.

"I had to relearn how to eat," he says.

Today he has dropped from 292 pounds to about 185. "I feel 100 percent better," he says. "I believe I've pleased God by taking care of my temple. God has taken care of all my medical problems. I believe God has blessed me because I decided to dedicate my temple to him and stop abusing it." (View Rob's story at www.ginghamsburg.org/mflresources.)

All leadership begins with self-leadership. All our excellence, our ability to influence people positively, begins there too. Our bodies are not our own. We are called to honor God with them. Until we exercise discipline over our bodies, our minds and spirits will be held hostage to our passions and appetites.

Have you had *your* conversion? Your life is a gift; your body is God's temple. Make your life and body an honorable, excellent offering to God through the discipline of healthy eating and exercise.

Rest Area Reflections

Read aloud the main Scripture, Psalm 128.

1. Although we all enjoy the gift of life, some may view a healthy lifestyle as optional. Consider adopting a healthy eating and exercise regimen for:
   • overall wellness
   • increased length of life
   • improved physical appearance
   • God's honor

2. This chapter names six factors affecting longevity. Where do you need to start?
   • attitude
   • mental activity
   • relationships
   • exercise
   • genes
   • diet

3. All leadership begins with self-leadership. What are positive and negative ways you've influenced people closest to you in regard to healthy lifestyle issues?

4. Share with someone else what God is saying to you.

work your program: thriving in life, influence, and mission

With you there is forgiveness,
so that we can, with reverence, serve you. (Ps. 130:4)

Followers of Jesus are on a lifelong ascent called transformation. Most people, however, come to church seeking relief rather than transformation. They are not prepared for the pain and exertion that accompany genuine life change. They choose not to look inside themselves for what God wants to change. It's easier to find an excuse and blame something or someone for whatever is wrong about life. Most prefer to mask pain instead of facing it, and humans will reach for work, entertainment, sex, chemicals, sports, people, and even religion to design the mask.

The root of all brokenness is self-absorption, the trap of presuming that "it's all about me." Self becomes the center of our reality. We search for meaning through the pursuit of happiness. We abandon the path of ascent to go after gods that promise to make us happy: toys, entertainment, or other stimulation, but to no avail. These false gods cannot satisfy the deep longing of our hearts.

Prepare for Reentry

I remember watching the Columbia space shuttle shatter as it reentered the Earth's atmosphere across the skies of Texas. In the follow-up investigation it was discovered that Mission Control had been aware that a small piece of the spacecraft had broken off during takeoff. They saw it, however, as only a minor flaw that would create no real problems. They grew even more confident in the days after launch, as the shuttle circled the earth and showed no further problems.

It was a false confidence.

The shuttle disaster is a metaphor for our personal lives. We're vaguely aware of small pieces of brokenness in our innermost being, but we live most of our days in denial, relying on our own resourcefulness. We can look good on the outside, but we have a false confidence. Reentry is coming, and destruction—physical, emotional, or spiritual—is a very real possibility. The end result is not just self-destructive. It can prove devastating to those within our networks of influence.

Time to Repent

The consequence of self-focus is self-reliance. "I can do it," we say. "I'm strong. I can change. I'll find momentum. I can achieve, acquire, and ascend, and I can do it all by myself." We believe in God and profess Jesus, but we live in denial of our need. Our illusion is that the good life is something we can attain for ourselves and by ourselves.

Our illusion is that the good life is something we can attain for ourselves and by ourselves.

How many of us have learned to separate the spiritual part of our lives from our daily work routines? We might explore devotional thoughts every morning before going to work but live the rest of the day in reliance upon self and our own resourcefulness. We ask God to help when we get into a sticky place or a tough spot, but go through most days hardly giving God a second thought. We sing "Amazing Grace," but don't realize our own great need for amazing grace. "I can do it on my own," we claim. "I can change any time I want. Knowing what is right enables me to do what is right."

When I am in a hurry to get someplace, I'll push the pedal until I'm flying along at up to eighty miles an hour. I drive differently when a police car is behind me. I'm careful, and I watch my mirrors. I look ahead, and if there is a bend in the road, I will slow up a little bit.

My motive is not to do what is right; my motive is to avoid getting a ticket. Why? I'm broken. Something in me knows what is right, but I can't do it, and even when I do manage to do right, my motives are wrong. That's why I need a Savior. True transformation requires a cross.

Name Your Junk

Anyone who has been in a twelve-step program knows that the first step in your recovery is to become aware of your brokenness and powerlessness. The first Beatitude says, "Blessed are the poor in spirit, for theirs is the kingdom of heaven" (Matt. 5:3). Following Jesus involves self-renunciation: admitting, "I am broken." It's the first step toward transformation.

We all must deal with the junk piles that accumulate around our busy lifestyles. They're like the piles in our homes, made up of everything we don't have time to deal with in the activities of daily life. We try to make the piles look pretty, cover them up, or move them from place to place, but it doesn't work. Eventually we must deal with our junk.

Our hearts are the dwelling place of Christ. Jesus and junk cannot share the same space; light and darkness cannot coexist. We dare not rationalize or procrastinate. We must admit our brokenness, acknowledging our sin before God. We cannot let any area of our hearts go unexposed; we must name our junk.

In Luke 15, Jesus tells the story of the awakening of the prodigal son. He is out there, self-reliant and self-sufficient. He loves his father, but he is disconnected from home. "When he came to his senses, he said, 'How many of my father's hired servants have food to spare, and here I am starving to death!' " When the prodigal son realizes his brokenness, he repents and names his junk. "I will set out and go back to my father, and say to him, 'Father, I have sinned against heaven and against you. I am no longer worthy to be called your son; make me like one of your hired servants'" (Luke 15:17-19). The son's brokenness informed his new identity: grateful servant. He represents a movement from self to servant.

Receive God's Forgiveness

Even before the prodigal son named his junk, the father was waiting with open arms. "So he got up and went to his father. But while he was still a long way off, his father saw him and was filled with compassion for him; he ran to his son, threw his arms around him and kissed him" (Luke 15:20). Likewise, God mercifully waits for us with open arms.

The second step of transformation is to receive God's forgiveness and mercy. "If we confess our sins, he is faithful and just and will forgive us our

sins and purify us from all unrighteousness"
(1 John 1:9). We are not in the father's
embrace because we deserve to be here or
because we earned our way; we are here
because of the cross. Be merciful to yourself
and receive God's forgiveness.

**Be merciful
to yourself
and receive
God's
forgiveness.**

Work Your Program

To move forward on the ascent, we must take intentional, disciplined
steps every single day. At Ginghamsburg we started a worship celebration
for people on the road to recovery. I marvel at the courage and intensity
of those who are seeking to radically change their lives. Once controlled
entirely by their addiction, these Jesus followers have named a set of daily
practices that they absolutely must carry out in order to survive and
thrive. It's their program of recovery, disciplines they work on every day
to assure that true change takes place.

You and I are no different. Each of us needs a program of recovery, a per-
sonalized combination of life practices
that will enable us to build momentum
for life, keeping us on an upward
climb. When any parts of this program
are neglected, we begin to plateau and
lose momentum. Worse, we begin to
downsize God's dream for our lives.

**Each of us needs
a program of
recovery . . . that
will enable us to
build momentum
for life.**

Your Own Song of Ascent

The practices based on the acronym D-R-I-V-E represent disciplines
for sustaining strategic focus, integrity, and personal health as a leader.
They are the elements that keep me moving with momentum toward
God's promised future and enable my influence on others to be rooted in
healthy self-discipline.

What will it take for you to sustain momentum today, tomorrow, and
into the unknown future? If you don't have a program, a model for living,
I invite you to use D-R-I-V-E for thirty days. Think of what a day could
look like if you could experience devotion to God and readiness for lifelong learning. How would it feel to know you were giving your best

128

toward <u>i</u>nvesting in key relationships, <u>v</u>isioning for the future, and <u>e</u>ating and <u>e</u>xercising for a long and healthy life?

Your path awaits; your ascent is possible. Commit to self-leadership, for you cannot effectively and positively influence others unless you are effectively leading yourself. Momentum for life will be your blessing as you faithfully live inside the disciplines of your program. Go in God's authority as you move forward in renewed personal health, integrity, and strategic focus.

Rest Area Reflections

Read aloud the main Scriptures, Matthew 5:3 and Luke 15:17-20.

1. Is there a junk pile in your house? Where is it?

2. Can you identify potentially cancerous cells in your heart that could multiply and grow if left unchecked?

3. The disease of sin requires each one of us to intentionally "work a program" of recovery to stay pure in heart. What program do you work?
   - a daily Bible study (such as *Transformation Journal*)
   - a twelve-step recovery program
   - an accountability partner or cell group
   - all of the above
   - I don't have a program

4. What are your next steps for further working your program?

appendix: resources to keep you growing

Ginghamsburg Resources

Web link: www.ginghamsburg.org/mflresources.

Momentum: Mass in Motion

Video: "The Nick Hoover Story"
Video: "Momentum for Luka"

Devotion to God

Transformation Journal Web link: www.mytj.org.

Readiness for Lifelong Learning

Video: On the Street, "What Are You Learning?"
Designing Worship, Kim Miller (Group Publishing, 2004)
Out on the Edge, Michael Slaughter (Abingdon Press, 1998)

Investing in Key Relationships

Video: Mike Berry/Medway Church, "The Measure of Greatness"
Video: "The Leland Sprecher Story"

Visioning for the Future

Video: "The Sudan Miracle Offering"
Video: "Fast for Famine"

Eating and Exercise for Life

Video: "Shopping with Carolyn"
Video: "What Is Your Program?"
Video: Rob Dauber, "The Temple"

More Resources from Ginghamsburg

Spiritual Entrepreneurs: 6 Principles for Risking Renewal, Michael Slaughter (Abingdon Press, 1994, 1995)

Out on the Edge: A Wake-up Call for Church Leaders on the Edge of the Media Reformation, Michael Slaughter (Abingdon Press, 1998)

Real Followers: Beyond Virtual Christianity, Michael Slaughter (Abingdon Press, 1999)

Handbook for Multisensory Worship, Volume 1, Kim Miller (Abingdon Press, 1999)

Handbook for Multisensory Worship, Volume 2, Kim Miller (Abingdon Press, 2001)

UnLearning Church: Just When You Thought You Had Leadership All Figured Out! Michael Slaughter with Warren Bird (Group Publishing, 2002)

Designing Worship: Creating and Integrating Powerful God Experiences, Kim Miller (Group Publishing, 2004)

Money Matters: Financial Freedom for All God's Children, Michael Slaughter with Kim Miller (Abingdon Press, 2006)

Ultimately Responsible: When You're in Charge of Igniting a Ministry, Sue Nilson Kibbey (Abingdon Press, 2006)

Web-empower Your Church: Unleashing the Power of Internet Ministry, Mark M. Stephenson (Abingdon Press, 2006)

Transformation Journal: A One Year Journey Through the Bible, edited by Sue Nilson Kibbey and Carolyn Slaughter (Abingdon Press, 2007)

Art & Soul Video Series, "Transformational Storytelling," www.ginghamsburgresources.com/as

On the Street Video Series, www.ginghamsburgresources.com/ots

notes

1. Momentum: Mass in Motion

1. Steve Watters, "Overcoming Cybersex Addiction," http://www.fam ily.org/married/romance/a0017698.cfm. See also http://internet-filter-review.toptenreviews.com/internet-pornography-statistics.html.

2. Anne Lamott, *Bird by Bird: Some Instructions on Writing and Life* (New York: Anchor Books, 1994), 21.

3. Ibid., 25.

4. Ibid., 19.

5. www.mytj.org.

2. Devotion to God

1. See Eugene Peterson, *A Long Obedience in the Same Direction: Discipleship in an Instant Society* (Downer's Grove, Ill.: InterVarsity Press, 1980).

2. Peg Tyre, "In Search of Something More," *O: The Oprah Magazine* (January 2005): 147.

3. http://www.barna.org/FlexPage.aspx?Page=BarnaUpdate&BarnaUpdate ID=124.

4. James Tunstead Burtchaell, *The Dying of the Light: The Disengagement of Colleges and Universities from Their Christian Churches* (Grand Rapids: Eerdmans, 1988), 329.

5. Ibid., 339.

6. *Transformation Journal* is a devotional resource we write annually at Ginghamsburg. One version has been published by Abingdon Press. See Sue Nilson Kibbey and Carolyn Slaughter, *Transformation Journal: A One Year Journey Through the Bible* (Nashville: Abingdon Press, 2007).

3. Readiness for Lifelong Learning

1. Bethany McLean and Peter Elkind, *The Smartest Guys in the Room: The Amazing Rise and Scandalous Fall of Enron* (New York: Portfolio, 2003), 3.

2. Ibid., 21.

3. Gordon MacDonald, *Ordering Your Private World* (Nashville: Thomas Nelson, 1997), 103.

4. Kim Miller, *Designing Worship: Creating and Integrating Powerful God Experiences* (Loveland, Colo.: Group Publishing, 2004), 137.

5. Mark Driscoll, *The Radical Reformission: Reaching Out without Selling Out* (Grand Rapids: Zondervan, 2004), 100.

6. Michael Slaughter, *UnLearning Church* (Loveland, Colo.: Group Publishing, 2002). The revised edition is due out from Abingdon Press in fall 2008.

7. Michael Slaughter, *Out on the Edge: A Wake-Up Call for Church Leaders on the Edge of the Media Reformation* (Nashville: Abingdon Press, 1998).

8. *Wall Street Journal*, Monday, 3 November 2000, R28-R29.

4. Investing in Key Relationships

1. Thornton Wilder, *Our Town* (New York: HarperPerennial, 1938, 1998), 108.

5. Visioning for the Future

1. Michael Slaughter, *Spiritual Entrepreneurs: Six Principles for Risking Renewal* (Nashville: Abingdon Press, 1995), 109-11; text slightly updated for readability and accuracy.

2. Walt Kallestad and Kirbyjon Caldwell, *Entrepreneurial Faith: Launching Bold Initiatives to Expand God's Kingdom* (Waterbrook, 2004), 109.

3. For documentation, do a Google or Yahoo search on these words (without the quotation marks): "enough food to feed the world United States." Scholars like Jeffrey Sachs, hailed by *Time Magazine* as one of the world's one hundred most influential people, argue that all the world's

poverty could be eliminated in our time. See his book *The End of Poverty: Economic Possibilities for Our Time* (New York: Penguin Books, 2005).

4. Rick Warren, *The Purpose-Driven Life* (Grand Rapids: Zondervan, 2002), 17.

6. Eating and Exercise for Life

1. Richard Corliss and Michael D. Lemonick, "How to Live to Be 100," *Time Magazine* (August 30, 2004): 103.

2. Ibid., 104.

3. "New Calculation: Obesity Now No. 7 Among Causes of Death," April 5, 2005, http://www.cnn.com/2005/HEALTH/diet.fitness/04/20/obesity.deaths.ap/index.html.

4. James Swierzbin, "Fighting Obesity in America," *Berkeley Beacon* (February 17, 2005), http://www.berkeleybeacon.com.

5. Michael D. Lemonick, "The Year of Obesity," *Time Magazine* (December 27, 2004).

6. "Warning: Obesity is the New Tobacco," *Australian News* (February 21, 2005).

7. "Cancer Linked to Choices," *Dayton Daily News* (December 2, 2004).

8. Kenneth H. Cooper, *Faith-Based Fitness* (Nashville: Thomas Nelson, 1995), 3-10.

9. Ibid.

10. Corliss and Lemonick, 103.

11. "Health for Life," *Newsweek* (January 17, 2005): 48.

12. Ibid.

13. Ibid., 61.

14. Robert G. Tuttle Jr., *John Wesley: His Life and Theology* (Grand Rapids: Zondervan, 1982), 31.

15. *West Ohio News* (June 25, 2004), 11.

16. Howard A. Snyder, "Holiness in Postmodernity: Holiness and the Five Calls of God," paper presented to the Asbury Theological Seminary community on November 11, 2004.